THE WAYSIDE INNS

ON THE

LANCASTER ROADSIDE

BETWEEN

PHILADELPHIA AND LANCASTER

METALMARK BOOKS

THE WAYSIDE INNS ON THE LANCASTER ROAD.

A SCENE ON THE LANCASTER TURNPIKE IN DAYS GONE BY.

The Wayside Inns

on the

Lancaster Roadside

between

Philadelphia and Lancaster

BY

JULIUS F. SACHSE, Litt.D.

*Librarian, Masonic Temple, Philadelphia: Member of American Philosophical Society,
American Library Association, American Historical Association, International
Congrès des Orientalistes, Historical Society of Pennsylvania, American
Jewish Historical Association, Pennsylvania-German Society,
Colonial Society of Pennsylvania, Quatuor Coronati,
London*

SECOND EDITION

LANCASTER, PA.
1912

Copyright, 1915
By JULIUS F. SACHSE

PRESS OF
THE NEW ERA PRINTING COMPANY
LANCASTER, PA.

CONTENTS.

FOREWORD.

A portion of this series of sketches of the old Wayside Inns on the Lancaster roadside, was originally published some thirty years ago in the *Village Record,* at West Chester, the county seat of Chester County, one of the three original Counties of Penn's Colony on the Delaware. These papers gave a description of the old Inns on the Lancaster turnpike, between the "Eagle" near the fourteenth milestone and the old "Ship" Tavern near the twenty-seventh milestone.

Many of these facts and incidents were gleaned from time to time, by the writer while yet a lad, dating back some sixty years or more, when an occasional Drove was not an unusual sight, upon the neglected highway—and some of the old Conestoga wagons, were still to be seen under the wagon shed on an adjoining farm.

To these sketches, a list has been added of all the Old Inns from the "Fish" at the Schuylkill Ferry to the "Swan" at Lancaster. Illustrated with photographs by the writer of such views of the Old Inns as were standing as late as 1886.

In the year 1912–13, these papers were printed as part XXIII of the "Narative and Critical History of the German Influence in the Settlement and Development of Pennsylvania" in the Proceedings of the Pennsylvania-German Society, and are now republished to meet a widespread demand.

ILLUSTRATIONS.

THE WAYSIDE INNS ON THE LANCASTER ROADSIDE.

IN provincial or colonial days the most important institution in our commonwealth, next to the church and school-house, was the wayside inn. Scattered as they were along the roadside throughout the province they were important beacons for the weary traveller, as well as a haven of rest and refreshment for the sojourner, whether farmer, drover, teamster or traveller upon business or pleasure bent. Many of these taverns or inns became important landmarks in both our social and political history, growing in the course of years from the lowly log tavern, to the stately stone turnpike inn of later years, in which important social functions were held. In many instances they were also polling places, and the meeting place of Masonic Lodges and similar organizations. Some also were favorite places for mass meetings and political rallies, where the candidates held forth, occasions upon which the barrel of hard cider was ever in evidence to slake the thirst of the prospective voter.

Many of these wayside inns in Pennsylvania became known throughout the land for their good cheer, cleanliness and hospitality. The hosts or landlords of these houses of the better class were almost invariably Germans or Pennsylvania-Germans, and the culinary department was supervised by the wife of the innkeeper.

Everyone of these wives was a *hausfrau* in every sense of the word. Upon her devolved not alone the culinary department but the care and oversight of the whole establishment, except the bar, stable yard, and supervision of the hostlers and reception of the guests, which fell to her husband the landlord.

The meals at these inns, such as the Spread Eagle and Warren presided over by the Pennsylvana-German matron, as served were entirely different from the fare set out in the houses kept by other nationalities, for instance where in the other wayside inns, even of the better sort, regular fare consisted of fried ham, cornbeef and cabbage, mutton and beef stews and mush and molasses, bread half rye and corn meal, with occasional rump steak and cold meats, and tea. In these Pennsylvania-German inns we had such dishes as *Kalbskopf* (mock turtle) soup redolent with the odor of Madeira; *Sauer braten* a favorite dish of the Fatherland; *Schmor braten* (beef a la mode); *Spanferkel* (sucking pig stuffed and roasted); *Kalbsbraten* (roast veal filled); *Hammelsbraten* (roast mutton); *Kuttlefleck* (soused tripe spiced); *Hinkel pie* (chicken pot pie); *Apfelklöse* (apple dumplings); *Bratwurst* (sausage); applecake, coffee cake with its coating of butter, sugar and cinnamon, and many other dishes unknown to their English competitors.

To conduct one of these stands in turnpike days required quite as much executive ability as is required to manage one of the pretentious hostelries of the present day. The proprietors in many cases were men of intelligence and prominence in the community; even members of Congress and State Representatives are to be found among their number.

So closely were the lines drawn between the classes of the stage tavern and the wagoner, that no stage tavern would on any account permit a teamster to put up there for the night, for if it became known that a wagoner had stopped there it would be considered a lasting disgrace and would result in the loss of the better class of patrons.

From the earliest days in our history there were sharply defined lines in these wayside inns, as each class catered for special custom. Thus those of the better class were known as "stage stands," inns where the travelling public by stage stopped for refreshment, meals, and sometimes rest over night. Here also the relays were changed. Next in the scale came the "wagon stands," taverns patronized by wagoners or teamsters: here they "put up" for the night, feeding their tired teams, and in many cases sleeping upon a bag of hay upon the floor of the bar-room or barn. Another class were the "drove stands," where special accommodations were to be had by the drovers for their cattle, which were here watered, fed or pastured, until they were again upon the hoof towards their desti-nation. Lastly, come the lowest class of the passing wayside inns, the "tap house," where the lowest class of the passing or resident public was catered to. These houses harbored such as none of the other classes would

entertain. The chief income of these "tap houses" came
from the sale of bad spirits or whiskey. They were
invariably kept by Irishmen.

In olden times all distances between cities and places
were computed from inn to inn. Thus by referring to
any old provincial almanac, tables like this will be found.

COPY OF AN OLD DISTANCE TABLE GIVING A LIST OF TAVERNS ON THE OLD
LANCASTER ROAD OR KING'S HIGHWAY, WHICH WAS THE PREDECESSOR
OF THE PHILADELPHIA AND LANCASTER TURNPIKE.

Philadelphia to	M.	Qts.	Prs.*
Colters Ferry............................	1	3	52
Black Horse..............................	6	0	16
Merion Meeting..........................	7	2	65
Three Tuns..............................	9	3	66
The Buck................................	11	0	42
The Plough..............................	13	3	48
Radnor Meeting..........................	14	0	87
Mills Tavern.............................	16	1	26
The Ball................................	19	3	62
Signe of Adr'l Warren....................	23	1	22
White Horse.............................	26	1	18
Downing Mill............................	33	1	4
The Ship................................	34	2	30
The Wagon..............................	41	0	0
John Miller at the Tun...................	47	1	50
Pequa Bridge............................	48	1	11
Dougles's Mill...........................	49	2	20
Widdow Caldwells "Hat".................	53	2	58
John Vernon's...........................	60	0	52
Conistoga Creek.........................	64	1	10
Lancaster Court House...................	66		

Another feature of these old inns of the days gone by
were their sign boards which swung and creaked in their
yoke, high upon a mast or pole set in the roadside. These
sign boards were all figurative and in some cases painted
by artists of note. The cause for the figurative feature
was twofold; first, they were more ornate and could be
better understood by the two different nationalites which

* Miles, quarters and perches.

made up our population than signs lettered in either German or English. Thus, take for instance, "The Black Bear"; a representation of this animal was known at once to either German or Irishman, while the words "Black Bear" would have troubled the former, while the latter certainly never would have recognized his stopping place if the sign board bore the legend: "Der Schwartze Bär." Secondly, but few of the teamsters or wagoners, irrespective of race, could read; nearly all had their orders to stop at certain houses, and they knew them by the sign board when they came to them. Then again, in some cases the name of the subject would be different in the High or Palatinate German dialect; thus, twelve miles from Philadelphia, there was a wagon stand upon whose sign board was painted a sorrel horse, and among the English-speaking teamsters the inn was known by that name; referring to a High German distance-table, we find it scheduled as "Braunes Pfed," the "Brown Horse." To the Palatinate wagoner, however, it was known as "Der Fuchs," "The Fox." This was not an isolated case, the inn often receiving a nickname which eventually found its way into the local distance tables.

Many of these signs were of a homely character, such as The Hat, The Boot, The Wagon, The Eagle, The Lion, The Cat, The Turk's Head, etc.

The drove stands usually had signs pertinent to their class of patrons, such as The Bull's Head, The Lamb, The Ram's Head, The Swan (black or white), etc.

The tap houses were known by such names as "The Jolly Irishman," "Fox Chase," "The Fiddler," "The Cat," etc.

The better class of inns or stage stands were usually named after popular heroes, such as "The King of Prussia," "St. George and the Dragon," "General Washington," "General Paoli," "Spread Eagle," and the "Indian Queen." The names were sometimes changed, owing to political changes; thus, one of the most noted taverns on the Lancaster roadside, the "Admiral Warren," after the Revolution had the coat on the figure of the sign board changed from red to blue, and henceforth it was "The General Warren," in honor of the hero of Bunker Hill. Similar cases are upon record where the head of "King George," after the struggle for Independence, was, by aid of the painter's brush, metamorphosed into "George Washington."

The highest development of the wayside inn was reached when the Lancaster turnpike became the chief highway and the model roadbed in the United States.

Pennsylvania merits unquestionably the praise of having contracted the first stone turnpike in this country. It led from Philadelphia to Lancaster, it was 62 miles long; was commenced in 1792, and finished in 1794, at an expense of $465,000, by a private company, and it became the pattern for all subsequent hard roads in this country.

Originally nine toll bars ("Schlagbaume") were erected between Philadelphia and Lancaster, at the following distances, beginning at two miles west of the Schuylkill, viz., 2, 5, 10, 20, 29½, 40, 49½, 58½, Witmer's Bridge.

The Lancaster turnpike replaced the old Conestoga or King's road, which connected Philadelphia with Lancaster, the chief inland city of Penn's colony.

The following is a copy of an old distance-table giving a list of the taverns and landmarks on the old Lancaster road or King's highway, which was the predecessor as it were of the turnpike:

Philadelphia to	M.	Qts.	Prs.
Colter's Ferry................................	1	3	52
Black Horse...................................	6	0	16
Merion Meeting..............................	7	2	65
Three Tuns...................................	9	3	66
The Buck.....................................	11	0	42
The Plough...................................	13	3	48
Radnor Meeting..............................	14	0	87
Mills Tavern.................................	16	1	26
The Ball......................................	19	3	62
Sign of Adml. Warren......................	23	1	22
White Horse.	26	1	18
Downing Mill................................	33	1	4
The Ship......................................	34	2	30
The Wagon...................................	41	0	0
John Miller at the Tun....................	47	1	50
Pequa Bridge................................	48	1	50
Dougless Mill	49	2	20
Widow Colwell's "Hat"....................	53	2	58
John Vernon's...............................	60	0	52
Conestoga Creek............................	64	1	10
Lancaster Court House.....................	66		

It was the purpose of this series of papers* to give the history of some of these old public houses, land-marks as they were, both legendary and documentary, showing the developments from the earliest hostelry, the "Blue Ball," in Tredyffrin Township, Chester County, established half way between the Schuylkill river and Brandywine creek, when yet the pack-horse reigned supreme, to the multitude of public houses for the enter-tainment of man and beast, often so close together on the turnpike that several could be found within a mile.

How the roadside inns and taverns increased on the new road between Philadelphia and Lancaster upon the completion of the turnpike between these two points, owing to the great increase of travel, is best seen by a com-parison of the above list of the King's or "Old" road with a list compiled by the writer and appended to this paper, where it will be seen that the number of roadside

* 1886.

inns between the two cities had increased from fourteen
on the old road to fifty and more on the turnpike.

In this list are given some of the names by which these
landmarks were known to the German teamsters, drovers
or travellers of that day.

The hard stone road, its white surface glistening in the
sunlight, with its ever changing scene of life and activity,
formed a picturesque and diversified panorama. In later
days we have the Troy coach, swinging upon its leather
springs, rolling along the hard road, drawn by four prancing horses; the Conestoga wagon with its broad tires;
the slow-plodding six-horse team with tinkling yoke bells;
the large droves of cattle being driven from the green
pastures of Chester and Lancaster to the seaboard; the
accommodation stage-wagon in contrast to the mail coach,
and the farm wagon or "dearborn," with the farmer
going to or from the city market; and many other features
all contributed to this ever changing scene.

With the advent of the railroad with its iron horse the
scene changed until within a few years the various turnpikes virtually became deserted highways, giving up to
mere local travel—with road-bed neglected or abandoned
until in some cases they became dangerous to travel.

While the wayside inns, once so important a landmark,
gradually went out of existence, many of them struggling
for some time as country boarding houses, or degenerating
to the level of an ordinary country tavern, which in colonial times were places of importance, and now merely live
in the traditions of the county, and vaguely in the memory
of a few of a former generation still amongst us, it was
to perpetuate such records and traditions that the writer
gathered such as were available relating to the various
hostelries as were, or had been on the Lancaster road and

turnpike within the bounds of Chester County. These records, forming a series of papers, were published in the "Village Record" of Chester County during the "80's" of the last century.

The two following papers, "The Spread Eagle" and "The Warren" have been selected for republication in the PROCEEDINGS of the Pennsylvania-German Society, as these hostelries were strictly representative Pennsylvania-German houses, kept by the Siter and Fahnestock families respectively. These two houses, stage-stands of the first order, where "entertainment was dispensed for man and beast," had not only a local reputation for elegance, but a national one as well, during the former turnpike days, until supplanted by the state railroad from Philadelphia to Columbia about the year 1836.

What is true of the old Lancaster turnpike applies also to the roads leading out from Philadelphia to Bethlehem and the northeast, and to the road to Baltimore and the south; many of the hostelries on these roads were kept by Pennsylvania-Germans, or men of German birth.

Of late years, long after the following stories were written, a new factor appeared with the advent of the twentieth century, namely the horseless carriage, which has had an unexpected effect upon our old turnpikes, so sadly neglected for many years, and in certain localities abandoned as unfit for travel. The advent of this factor, with power derived from gasoline, electricity or denatured alcohol, brought about a demand for good roads. The agitation for safe roads spread over the land, and resulted in many delapidated and neglected turnpikes being again surfaced and put in good condition for safe and speedy travel; among these reconstructed roads there is none finer than the Lancaster Turnpike from Philadelphia, through

2

what is known as the suburban district on the Pennsylvania main line; and it is now again, as it was when first built over a century ago, quoted as the model and specimen piece of road building, second to none in the state.

Whether this new condition of travel will eventually bring about the rehabilitation of any of our old colonial hostelries in a manner suitable to the needs of the twentieth century, or whether they will be supplanted by establishments like those at Bryn Mawr or Devon, remains to be seen.

In the meantime, these sketches of days gone by may prove of interest to the autoists, both male and female, as they gaily spin up or down the old highway, in a luxury and speed undreamed of by the old wagoner, teamster or stagers of a century ago.

THE WAYSIDE INNS ON THE LANCASTER ROAD.

THE "RED LION" HOTEL (No. 10).

NEAR THE SEVENTH MILE STONE, IN THE VILLAGE OF ARDMORE.

FROM AN OLD PHOTOGRAPH SHOWING A PUBLIC VENDUE.

FROM THE "FISH" WEST OF THE SCHUYL-KILL TO THE "SWAN" AT LANCASTER.

IN the old distance tables published prior to the building of the Philadelphia and Lancaster Turnpike the distances are given from the court house formerly at Second and Market streets. This course was followed in the early days of the turnpike. The milestones on the turnpike, however, commence from the Schuylkill River. Consequently in the later distance tables the locations of the old landmarks appear to be two miles less than on the older tables, the two miles being the distance from the court house to the west bank of the Schuylkill.

The following list of inns on the Lancaster turnpike is based on notes made by the writer during the year 1886–1887, when most all of the photographs were taken.

Many of these old landmarks have been changed since that time; some remodeled for the use of wealthy suburban residents; others, half in ruin, are occupied by foreign laborers; some have been demolished, and a few have descended to the level of an ordinary country tavern.

In compiling this list every effort has been made to give the proper location of the various old wayside inns between Philadelphia and Lancaster.

Shortly after the turnpike and the permanent, or Market Street bridge, over the Schuylkill was completed, the stage coaches started on their journey from the corner of Eighth and Market streets.

The traveller after crossing the Market Street (permanent) bridge over the Schuylkill at Philadelphia, on his journey westward, first passed:

1. **The Fish,** on the west side of the Schuylkill, which was kept by the Boone family.

2. **The Lamb Tavern,** built and kept by John Elliot. The exact location of this old inn is not known.

3. **The Rising Sun.** This was in Blockley Township, about two and a half miles west of the bridge.

4. **The Columbus Tavern,** built in 1798, by Col. Edward Heston for his son Abraham. It stood on the turnpike in Blockley Township, just east of Meetinghouse Lane, the present 52d Street.

5. **The White Lamb.** Opposite the fourth mile stone near the present Wynnefield Avenue. This building is still standing.

In this vicinity, in later years there were several taverns of minor importance, which are not to be included in our list of the Wayside Inns. They were known as:

HUGHES TAVERN.

THE DURHAM OX.

LUDWICKS.

SHEEP DROVE YARD.

These have long since passed away, nor can the

THE WAYSIDE INNS ON THE LANCASTER ROAD.

THE BUCK TAVERN MILLERS (No. 13).

ONE-FOURTH MILE WEST OF THE EIGHTH MILE STONE, AS IT APPEARED IN 1912.

exact location be given with certainty at the present day.

6. **The Flag Tavern.** This was the first inn on the turnpike in Lower Merion Township, Montgomery County. The College of St. Charles Borromeo now covers part of the site. Near the fifth milestone.

7. **The Black Horse Tavern.** Also in lower Merion, Montgomery County, about four miles west of the river. It is said that the original Black Horse Inn was built on the old Lancaster road by a progenitor of the Wynne family. This is about one mile east of the old Friends Merion Meeting-house just over the city line.

8. **The Three Tuns.** In Lower Merion Township, Montgomery County, about two miles above Merion Meeting, seven miles from Philadelphia.

9. **The Green Tree.** In same township, about half a mile west of the Three Tuns.

10. **The Red Lion.** Also in Ardmore. This inn was for many years kept by the Litzenberg family. It is still kept at the present day as a saloon and tavern. It is about a quarter of a mile west of the seventh milestone.

11. **The Seven Stars.** In the village of Athensville, now Ardmore, also in Lower Merion, Montgomery County. Kept for many years by the Kugler family. It was upon the south side of the turnpike, near the seventh milestone.

12. **The Prince of Wales.** In Haverford Township, Delaware County. About half a mile west of Ardmore.

13. **The Buck Tavern.** On the south side of the turnpike, between Haverford and Bryn Mawr, in Haverford Township, Delaware County, ¼ mile west of

the eighth milestone, on the extreme verge of the
county.   This inn was a stage stand of the first order,
and was renowned for its good cheer.   It was kept
for many years by the Miller family, and was appointed a post-tavern at an early day.   In 1832
Jonathan Miller, the tavern keeper, was the postmaster.

14. **The Sorrel Horse.**   In Radnor Township, Delaware
County.

15. **The Plough.**   Also in Radnor township.   In later
years, after being remodeled, became the residence
of a Philadelphia capitalist.   The location is about
eleven miles west of the Schuylkill.

16. **The Unicorn.**   Also known as "Miles Tavern,"
after the family who kept it for many years.   It was
also known as the "Irish" Tavern.   The location
of this old hostelry was a short distance below the
fourteenth milestone on the turnpike, where both the
old road and turnpike cover the same ground.

   [*Note.*   These three taverns—the Sorrel Horse,
Plough, and Unicorn—all appear as landmarks on
the old Lancaster road.   Also on the early distance
tables of the turnpike this would lead to the inference
that at least the Sorrel Horse and Plough were re-
opened on the pike.]

17. **The Spread Eagle.**   Radnor Township, Delaware
County, on the border of Chester County, a few rods
above the fourteenth milestone on the turnpike.
This was a stage stand of the first order, and renowned for its cleanliness and good cheer.   It was
a post tavern and relay station.   For many years this
inn was kept by the Siter family.   The hamlet of
eight or ten dwellings and shops that grew up around

THE WAYSIDE INNS ON THE LANCASTER ROAD.

THE "BLUE BALL" (No. 22), NEAR 17TH MILESTONE.   "DROVE" TAVERN (No. 21), OPPOSITE 16TH MILESTONE.
"SPRING HOUSE" (No. 20), BET. 15TH AND 16TH MILESTONE.   "STAGE" TAVERN (No. 19), NEAR 15TH MILESTONE.

Edward Siter was the postmaster. During the eighth decade of last century, the property was bought by the Drexel and Childs operation at Wayne and demolished.

18. **The Lamb Tavern.** The first inn on the turnpike in Chester County. It stood a short distance east of the fifteenth milestone, and was kept by the Lewis family. Many of the reminiscences of this vicinity were told the writer by George Lewis, then in his ninetieth year.

19. **The Stage Tavern.** On the hillside a little west of the fifteenth milestone. It was located upon what was claimed to be the highest point west of Philadelphia. Here the town of Glassly was laid out about the year 1800. The old inn was a wagon and drove stand, and was kept by the Beaumont family.

20. **The Spring House.** In the hollow, just east of Reeseville, now Berwyn. Kept for a time by a branch of the Kugler family. It was between the fifteenth and sixteenth milestones. In later years it was known as Peggy Dane's. The site is now covered by an artificial ice and cold storage plant.

21. **The Drove Tavern.** In Tedyffrin Township, Chester County, opposite the sixteenth milestone. It was kept by the Reese family, from which the settlement took its original name "Reeseville," now the flourishing town of Berwyn. The old signboard is now in the Pennsylvania Historical Society.

22. **The Blue Ball.** Prissy Robinson's, on the turnpike near the seventeenth milestone, now known as Daylesford. For years this old inn was kept by the notorious Prissy Robinson, who for years was a local character in this locality.

23. **The Black Bear.** For a time known as the Bull's

Head.   This old inn stood on the south side of the turnpike where the road from Newtown Square to Howelville crosses the turnpike.   It was a wagon and drove stand during the turnpike days and was torn down in 1877.   The barn stood on the southwest corner of the road.

24. **The General Jackson** later **The Franklin.**   On the north side of the turnpike at the eighteenth milestone. This old inn, still standing, was kept for years by a branch of the Evans family.   Prior to the Antimasonic craze (1828–1832), the inn was known as a lodge stand, as a special room was set apart for society meetings, among which was "Farmer's Lodge, No. 183, Free and Accepted Masons," who met there from 1822 until about 1830.   This inn is in Trydeffrin Township, Chester County.

25. **The Paoli.**   Another of the celebrated stage stands on the eastern end of the turnpike.   It was in Trydeffrin Township, Chester County, on the north side of the turnpike, just west of the eighteenth milestone.   For many years it was kept by the Davis and later by the Evans family.   It was the polling place for several townships, also the chief postoffice for this district.   Samuel Davis was the postmaster in 1832.   In later years the Paoli was used as a summer boarding house, presided over by Joshua Evans and Mrs. Davis.   It was destroyed by fire some twenty odd years ago.

26. **The Green Tree.**   Near the nineteenth milestone in Willistown Township, Chester County.   This was a wagon stand in the early days.   Its last boniface was Davis Gill, sheriff of the county.   It was demolished in 1877 when the Pennsylvania Railroad was straightened.

27. **The Warren Tavern** [Admiral Vernon, Admiral Warren, General Warren]. In East Whiteland Township, Chester County, on the north slope of the South Valley Hill. It was near the twentieth milestone, and the first inn on the turnpike in the Great Chester Valley. It was one of the oldest inns west of Philadelphia, being on the King's Road in Provincial days, twenty-two miles west of the court house in Philadelphia. After the Revolution it was kept by a branch of the Fahnestock family from Ephrata, during whose régime its reputation was second to none in the state. In 1832 Charles Fahnestock was the postmaster. They were also the first innkeepers who refused to sell liquors on the Sabbath.

28. **General Wayne.** A wagon stand, near the twenty-second milestone, at the north side of the turnpike. On the inside of the barroom door the marks of the teamsters' whips could be seen, where, in former years, they tried their strength, and the cutting power of their whip lashes. This building is now used as a dwelling.

29. **The Steamboat.** On the north side of the turnpike, half a mile east of the twenty-fourth milestone. It is in West Whiteland Township, near the present Glen Lock Station on the Pennsylvania Railroad. At present writing the house is unoccupied and fallen into decay.

30. **The Sheaf of Wheat** [Sheaf—Barley Sheaf]. A wagon and drove stand near the twenty-sixth milestone.

31. **The Ship Tavern.** Near the twenty-seventh milestone in West Whiteland Township. Originally west of Downingtown, at a point where the Old Lan-

caster road and the new turnpike occupied the same
ground. When the original *ship* was closed, the
old sign was taken to the new location, and there for
many years swung and creaked in its yoke by the
roadside.

32. **The General Washington.** In East Caln Township,
near the thirty-first milestone. Also known as *Downings* or the *Stage office* and on the old distance tables
as *Downing's Mill,* thirty-three miles from the Philadelphia court house. This noted hostelry was at the
eastern end of the village of Downingtown, on the
north side of the turnpike at the junction of the Lion-
ville road. This inn was the halfway station between Philadelphia and Lancaster, and occupied the
same position on the successive roads between those
two points. "Downings" was a "stage" stand of
the first order. It is not known what effigy the
signboard bore during provincial days. After the
Revolution, however, it became known as the "General Washington," and the swinging sign portrayed
the general and a civilian standing side by side. In
early days this inn was also a postoffice. Isaac
Downing was the postmaster in 1832. The building
is now remodelled and used as a private residence

33. **The Halfway House.** A wagon stand on the south
side of the turnpike, a short distance west of "Downings." The site of this old inn is now occupied by
several store buildings.

34. **The Swan Tavern.** Also in Downingtown. It is
on the south side of the turnpike, a short distance
west of the above two hostelries. The old *Swan*
has of late been remodeled and is now the chief
tavern and saloon in East Downingtown.

THE "GENERAL WASHINGTON" (No. 32).
BETTER KNOWN AS "DOWNING'S."
NEAR THE 31ST MILESTONE, NOW (1912) A PRIVATE RESIDENCE.

35. **Gallagherville Tavern.** On the turnpike, near the thirty-third milestone.

36. **The Ship Tavern.** The original *Ship* Tavern was on the south side of the turnpike in West Whiteland Township, Chester County, about one mile west of Downingtown, near the thirty-second milestone, at a point where the old Lancaster or Conestoga road and the new turnpike occupied the same ground. When the original tavern was closed, the old sign was taken to the new location, near the twenty-seventh milestone, where for many years it swung and creaked in its yoke by the roadside, perforated as it was by the bullet holes made by continental soldiers during the Revolution. The original building is still standing, being used as a summer residence. Thomas Parke was the proprietor during Revolutionary times, and later was acquired by the Edge family.

37. **The Prussian Eagle.** On the east bank of the West Branch of the Brandywine, in Valley Township, now the flourishing town of Coatesville. In 1860 the inn was kept by J. T. Minster, since which time it has been enlarged and is now known as the "Speakman House." It is west of the thirty-sixth milestone.

38. **The Midway House.** Formerly on the turnpike just beyond the West Branch of the Brandywine. It was just east of the thirty-seventh milestone. The inn took its name from the fact that it was just half way or midway between Philadelphia and Columbia, the original termini of the old state railroad. In 1860 it was kept by A. Bear. Henry Conroy was also a former innkeeper.

39. **Hand's Pass.** (*The Cross Keys.*) This old inn, a wagon stand, was so named after its location. It

stood in what was in former days a wild and lonely spot on the hill side, then covered with heavy timber. It was near the thirty-eighth milestone. Tradition tells us that it received its name from the fact that General Hand had encamped there with a portion of Washington's army. The old hostelry was surrounded by a dense wood, and for some reason had an uncanny reputation, so much so that many teamsters avoided remaining there over night as much as possible. There were also a number of ghostly traditions current about this old inn during turnpike days.

40. **The Rainbow Tavern.** Between the thiry-eighth and thirty-ninth milestone. This was also a wagon and drove stand.

41. **The Barley Sheaf.** Noted on the distance table in Carey's Almanac for 1803 as being eight miles west of Downingtown. This would be near the thirty-ninth milestone.

42. **The Washington Tavern.** West of the fortieth milestone.

43. **The States Arms** (also United States Arms). This inn was in Sadsbury Township, on the north side of the turnpike, at the intersection with the road leading from the Conestoga and Pequea country to Wilmington. This inn, in the early years of the nineteenth century, was the last tavern in Chester County, where stages going west changed horses. The old inn was also known as a "lodge" stand, as here at the beginning of last century "Unity" Masonic Lodge, No. 80, held its meetings. It was between the fortieth and forty-first milestones.

THE WAYSIDE INNS ON THE LANCASTER ROAD.

THE "STEAMBOAT" (No. 29),
BETWEEN 23D AND 24TH MILESTONE.
THE "GREEN TREE" (No 26),
NEAR 19TH MILESTONE.

TOLL BOOTH NEAR MALVERN.
THE "GENERAL JACKSON" (FRANKLIN), (No. 24),
AT 18TH MILESTONE.

44. **Sadsbury Hotel.** Also known as *Kendig's*, formerly as *Baer's*. Just east of the forty-first milestone, at the intersection of the Wilmington Pike. This inn was also one of the tavern postoffices. In 1832 John Kendig was the postmaster. At the present day it is used as a country tavern.

45. **The Black Horse Tavern.** Near the forty-second milestone in West Sadsbury Township. This inn was also used as a postoffice. In 1832 Samuel Jackson was the postmaster. House now owned by John Wallace Boyd.

46. **The General Wayne Tavern.** At the forty-third milestone. At the close of the war of 1812 John Petit was the owner of the Wayne with fifty acres of land. Being beautifully situated a company was formed to lay out a town in 1814. Petit sold his tavern and farm to Abraham & Company for $16,000, whereon they laid out a town and called it "Moscow." The turnpike became Cossack street for the nonce, while parallel and cross streets were given Russian names. The plot was gotten up in fine style, but flourished only on paper. After the bubble bursted the tavern property became the celebrated Moscow Academy, for many years presided over by Rev. ———. Latta. The milestone in front of this house is the first giving the distance both ways, viz., 43 m. to P.; 19 m. to L.

47. **The Cross Keys.** A wagon stand near the forty-fourth milestone from Philadelphia, the eighteenth from Lancaster.

48. **The Mount Vernon.** In Sadsbury Township, Lancaster County, between the forty-fifth and forty-sixth milestones, a short distance west of the Chester

County line. The inn is still kept as a licensed house, and stands at the intersection of the road leading from Christiana to Limeville.

49. **Clemson Tavern.** *"The Continental."* Formerly west of the forty-seventh milestone. This was also known as the "Gap Tavern." The house stood on the north and the barn on the south side of the tavern; and it was currently reported there was a tunnel leading from one to the other. It was the rendezvous of the notorious "Gap gang" broken up by the conviction of Amos Clemson, who died in prison, and others of its leaders.

50. **The Rising Sun.** Also known as *"The Sign of the Rising Sun"* and *"The Sign of the Rising of the Sun."* A tavern on the turnpike near the forty-eighth milestone at the crossing of the pike by the Newport road. The locality is still known as the Gap. The inn was a wagon stand for the teamster and wagoner. In 1801 it was kept by John Young, and for a time was the meeting place for a Masonic Lodge.

51. **Slaymaker's Tavern.** A noted stage stand and post house, on the north side of the turnpike between the forty-eighth and forty-ninth milestone. It was kept by a family from which it took its name. Amos Slaymaker was a member of the firm of Reeside & Slaymaker, who operated a line of stages on the turnpike before the time of railroads. In 1832 Wm. D. Slaymaker was the local postmaster.

52. **Kinzer's Tavern.** Between the forty-ninth and fiftieth milestone.

53. **Williamstown.** Between the fifty-first and fifty-second (tenth and eleventh) milestone, now known as The Vintage and is an ordinary country tavern.

THE RISING SUN TAVERN (No. 50).

NEAR THE 48TH MILESTONE, AS IT APPEARED IN 1912.

PHOTOGRAPHED BY J. D. HASTINGS, ESQ., 1912.

54. **The Plow and Anchor.** At Leaman Place between the fifty-second and fifty-third milestone (ninth and tenth). This Tavern was kept for many years by John Reynolds, an ancestor of General John F. Reynolds. The old inn is now the residence of Miss Mary Leaman, who still treasures the signboard of the old inn.

55. **Paradise Tavern.** Near the fifty-third (ninth) milestone.

56. **Soudersburg Tavern.**

57. **Geiger's Tavern.**

58. **The Running Pump.** Near the fifty-fifth (seventh) milestone, on what is now known as the Buckwalter farm.

59. **Greenland Tavern.** West of Mill Creek, between the fifty-eighth and fifty-ninth (third and fourth) milestone.

60. —— **Tavern.** (Bridgeport.) East end of Witmer's Bridge over Conestoga River.

61. **"Conestoga Inn" Tavern.** West bank of Conestoga River at Witmer's Bridge.

62. **The Swan at Lancaster.** Kept by Col. Matthias Slough from 1761 to 1806. This noted tavern was built in 1754. This inn was a stage stand of the first order, and was the scene of many important gatherings, social, political and Masonic. The regular meetings of Lodge No. 43, F. & A. M., being held at the Swan Tavern from June, 1788, until June, 1792.

OLD INNS ON THE LANCASTER ROAD SIDE.

THE SPREAD EAGLE TAVERN NEAR THE 14TH MILESTONE

IN the extreme northwestern part of Radnor township, in Delaware county, on the Lancaster Turnpike, fourteen miles west of Philadelphia, formerly stood at the base, as it were, of the South Valley Hill, a large three-story stone building with porch and piazza extending along the entire front.

By the date stone, high up in the gable the wayfarer could still plainly see the year when the house was completed, the legend read "1796." This building, one of those monuments by which we may be able to trace the past, was formerly the justly celebrated "Spread Eagle Tavern," known far and wide to travellers from both continents; built, as the stone informs us, in the year following the one in which was completed the first link of

FROM AN OLD ENGRAVING

THE OLD SPREAD EAGLE INN (No. 17).

ON THE LANCASTER ROADSIDE PRIOR TO TURNPIKE DAYS.

what was to be the first great National highway to the West, and at the date of the building of the Inn connected Philadelphia, then the Capitol City of the United States, with Lancaster, the second important town of the Commonwealth, and it may here not be amiss to say that to Pennsylvania's private citizens who subscribed almost half a million dollars to complete this great work of internal improvement, belongs unquestionably the praise of having constructed the first stone turnpike in the Union.

The turnpike at this point for a short distance occupies the bed of the old Provincial or King road. The present building supplanted a small rude stone house, which was kept as a house of entertainment by one Adam Ramsower as early as 1769. The following year he petitioned to have his license renewed. In his petition to the Court August 28, 1770, he says: "Your Honors hath been pleased for these several years past to grant me your recommendation to the Governor for a license to keep a public house of entertainment," &c. Anthony Wayne appears as one of the subscribers to this petition.

The following year Ramsower advertised the place for sale as shown by the following advertisement in a Philadelphia newspaper:—

"To be Sold

on Thursday the 26th of December instant A Valuable messuage, plantation and tract of land, situate in Radnor Township, Chester County adjoining the Lancaster road, Containing near 100 Acres of good land, about 16 miles from Philadelphia, about 70 acres are cleared and the remainder exceedingly well timbered about 14 acres of very good watered meadow, and an excelent Orchard that bears plentifully every year; the dwelling house is a large well

3

finished stone building, and a well accustomed tavern, known by the name of the "Spread Eagle" and is well accommodated with a barn, stables, sheds, gardens &c a pump of good water near the door, with trough to water creatures.   Any person inclining to purchase may come and view the premises before the day of Sale, at which time the Conditions of Sale will be made known by

"ADAM RAMSOWER."

(*Pennsylvania Gazette,* Dec. 19, 1771.)

The next official knowledge we have of the tavern is the following curious petition, together with the quaint "certificate of character" which accompanied it when handed into Court.

"To the Worshipful Justices of Court of General Quarter Sessions of the Peace, held and Kept at Chester the 25th day of August, 1772:

"The petition of Jacob Hinkel of Said County, Humbly Sheweth:

"That your petitioner hath lately purchased the messuage and plantation where Adam Ramsower lately dwelt, situated in Radnor township, in said county, at which place a house of public entertainment hath been kept for a number of years past, known by the name of 'Spread Eagle;' your petitioner therefore prays that your honors will be pleased to grant him a recommend to his honor, the Governor, for a license to keep a public house of entertainment at the place aforesaid and your petition shall pray.

JACOB HINKEL."

"LANCASTER COUNTY SS.

"Whereas, Jacob Hinkel, tanner, the bearer hereof, who hath resided within the County for the term of 12 years, is now moving to Chester county with the intention to keep a house of public entertainment on the road leading from Philadelphia to Lancaster at the noted tavern of the 'Spread Eagle' and whereas, the said Jacob Hinkel did petition to us subscribing magistrates and other inhabitants of Lancaster county for a testimony of his character whilst he lived in the said county, and also for a recommendation to the magistrates of said county of Chester.

"This is therefore to certify that the said Jacob Hinkel whilst he lived in said county acted the parts of a true and honest member of the civil government, and as such by virtue of our underwritten names, we do heartily recommend him to the worshipful, the Judges of the Peace of the County of Chester, etc, etc.

EDWARD SHIPPEN,
EMANUEL CARPENTER,
JAMES CLEMSON,
and ten others,

Lancaster, the fourth day of August, 1772."

At the commencement of the Revolutionary period the house was known as the gathering place of the patriots of the vicinity, while "Miles" old tavern, a short distance below, which had been rechristened "The Unicorn" and was then kept by a loyal Irishman, was patronized by the citizens who were either Tory or Loyalists.

During the alternate occupation of this territory by the opposing forces 1777–8, the house became somewhat of a land mark, several reports and letters in reference to the military situation being dated at, or mentioning the "Spread Eagle" tavern. During the encampment of the American army at Valley Forge the inn for a time was used as an outpost, where the large chestnut tree on the West side of the Valley road, about fifty feet North of the present turnpike, was utilized as a signal station, or outlook for that picket; this tree still standing (1886) may easily be recognized on the road leading to the present railroad station; it also marks the boundary line between Delaware and Chester counties.

The inn continued in the possession of Jacob and Daniel Hinkel until 1778 and possibly until 1781, although no records are known to exist, stating who kept the house between those years. We know that one Alexander Clay was in charge, from 1787 until 1791, when Adam Siter appears, and he was followed by John Siter, during whose time the new house was built.

As soon as the turnpike was finished it at once became the main artery of travel between the East and West. As the line of the new road at some points deviated a considerable distance from the old provincial road many of the colonial inns which had been landmarks for a century became useless on account of their distance from the new turnpike, others which were still accessible did not come up to the needs or demands of the increased travel brought forth by the new state of affairs.

Of the numerous inns which were at once projected and built along the line of the new thoroughfare, the "Spread Eagle" Tavern was one of the largest as well as the most pretentious public houses between Philadelphia and Lancaster.

The first sign board of the tavern was supported by two tall masts planted on the south side of the road; and is said to have been painted by one of America's most distinguished artists. It was a representation of the outspread American eagle as depicted on the silver dollar of that date with the shield of the Union on its breast, the wings extended, and grasping in one talon the arrows of war, while in the other the olive branch of peace; a blue scroll in his beak with the emblazoned legend "E Pluribus Unum" and thirteen stars for an event completed the gorgeous sign of the new candidate for the patronage of the traveling public.

Shortly after Martin Slough's successful attempt in 1795 to run a four-horse stage between Philadelphia and Lancaster, stage coach lines continued to increase on the new road, and the Spread Eagle at once sprang into popularity with the traveling public, as well as with the "wagoners" and "teamers"; for at that early day the furnishings and cuisine of the hostelry were probably unsurpassed in the State. It is said that during the summer and fall of 1798 when the Capitol city was again visited by the yellow fever scourge, our inn was crowded with members of the Government, as well as attaches of the accredited representatives of the foreign powers in Philadelphia.

It was not long before quite a hamlet grew up in the vicinity of the busy inn, besides the usual blacksmith and wheelwright shops, livery stable, barns and other outbuildings attendant to an inn of the first rank. There was a flourishing saddlery as well as a village cobbler and tailor. The large "Eagle" store on the opposite side of the turnpike still does a flourishing trade to this day. A post-office was located here at an early day and the hamlet became known to the world and on the maps and gazetteers of the day as "Sitersville."

The inn on account of its distance from the city became the stopping place of both mail, post and accommodation stages for meals and relays, it being the first station west and the last relay station eastward.

It also was the usual breakfast station for the stages leaving Philadelphia at four and five o'clock in the morning.   In 1807 the price charged stage passengers was 31¼ cents per meal while others were only charged 25 cents. The reason given for this discrimination was, that being obliged to prepare victuals for a certain number of passengers by the stage, whether they came or not, it frequently caused a considerable loss of time, and often a waste of victuals, whereas in the other case they knew to a certainty what they would have to prepare.

The expense of traveling by the stages from Philadelphia to Pittsburg at this period was $20 and 12½ cents for every pound of luggage beyond fourteen.   The charges, by the way, for meals and lodging were about $7. The whole distance was 297 miles, and was performed in six days.

The expense by wagon was $5 per cwt. for both persons and property, and the charges by the way amounted to about $12.   It would take twenty days or more to perform the journey by wagon.

The favorite liquid refreshments dispensed over the bar and drank by the hardy "wagoners" and travelers in these early times besides whisky, brandy, rum and porter, were such as "cyder" plain, royal or wine; "apple" and "peach" brandy; "cherry bounce," &c.   Among the better class of stage travelers a good bowl of "punch" was always in order and never out of order.

It is not known just how long John Siter remained in charge.   He was succeeded by Edward Siter, who for two years retired from the old inn, as is shown by following advertisement.

THE "SPREAD EAGLE" TAVERN (No. 17).

NEAR THE FOURTEENTH MILE STONE.

VIEW FROM SOUTHWEST.

VIEW FROM SOUTH.

REAR VIEW FROM NORTHEAST.

" EDWARD SITER

Late of the Spread Eagle on the Philadelphia and Lancaster Turnpike road, takes the liberty of informing his friends and the public in general that he has taken that large store on South East corner of Market and Eighth Sts Number 226 in Philadelphia where he is now opening a good assortment of groceries, wholesale and retail on the most reasonable terms, where country produce will be bought or stored and sold on commission with punctuality.

He believes himself from his former conduct in business to obtain a share of publick patronage."

(*Federalist,* Dec. 9, 1812.)

Edward Siter was succeeded by James Watson for two years. But the venture of neither proving successful we find Edward Siter again in charge of the inn until the year 1817.

The following five years—1817 to 1823—David Wilson, jr., was the host. Zenas Wells kept the inn 1823, 1824 and 1825.

For a short time during the first quarter of the century, most probably while the house was in charge of Wilson or Wells, a change was made on the old signboard, another neck and head being added by a local artist, thus changing our glorious bird of freedom into one of those nondescript birds with two heads as used in ancient heraldry; this change is still fresh in the memory of several octogenarians who yet live in the vicinity. It is further said that this change was caused by some political excitement rife at that time. The new signboard, however, caused much merriment among the neighbors and wagoners, who could not see the utility of the change, and by them the house was nicknamed the " Split Crow," and in an article written about 65 years ago by Mr. George W.

Lewis (still living) the house is referred to by that name.
After Edward W. Siter came in possession, in 1825, the
signboard was again Americanized, and after being re-
painted remained until it was finally effaced by the action
of the elements about the time the usefulness of the house
as an inn had passed away.

Among the curious customs pevalent at this time, was
for the smiths to burn their own charcoal, and it was not an
uncommon sight for the traveler to see a charcoal kiln on
fire back of the shops.

The continuing increase of travel and patronage soon
necessitated the erection of more taverns; it is said they
eventually averaged about one to the mile between the
Eagle and Downingtown. The first of these new turnpike inns stood about three quarters of a mile west of the
Eagle, on the eastern end of what was then known as the
"Glassley Commons."   The inn was known as the
"Lamb"; it was established by John Lewis about 1812
or 13, who remained there for two years, when he was
succeeded by the "Clingers," father and son, who remained in charge until the necessity for a public house
there had passed away.

A few hundred rods east of the Eagle where the old
road intersects the turnpike stood an old provincial inn,
"The Unicorn." This house was built in 1747 by one
James Miles. A license was granted to him in the following year. This inn was known on the early distance
tables as "Miles Tavern," being 16 miles, 1 qr., 26 perches
from the Court House in Philadelphia on the road to
Lancaster, and is noted on the quaint pamphlet published
by Wm. Bradford in Philadelphia in 1751. This building is no doubt still recollected by the residents of the township; also its destruction by fire on St. Valentine night,

February, 1872, attended unfortunately by the loss of a life, an old man being burned to death in the attempt to save some of his effects.

These two taverns just mentioned took most of the overflow which could not be accommodated at the Spread Eagle, still it is yet within the recollection of many persons when the yards of all three inns were filled to their utmost capacity with wagons, stages and teams, while the barrooms within resounded with the roystering song or ribald jests of the hardy wagoner.

The travel on the turnpike reached its height probably during the latter part of the '20's, just previous to the building of the Philadelphia & Columbia Railroad by the Canal Commissioners of the State. During this era all was life and bustle about the Inn; there was hardly a moment during the twenty-four hours of the day that there was not some travel past the Inn. It was a frequent sight to see long lines of Conestoga wagons going towards the city loaded with the products of the West or going in the opposite direction freighted with the productions of Eastern mills or foreign merchandise; these wagons were usually drawn by five stout horses, each horse having on its collar a set of bells consisting of different tones, which made very singular music as the team trudged along at the rate of about four miles an hour. Emigrants could also frequently be seen on their way, generally in companies for mutual assistance, going with their families and worldly possessions towards the new West—there to settle and found homes for their posterity. Large herds and flocks also furnished their quota to this ever moving living panorama.

Within the tavern all would be life and animation, on warm, fair nights the porch as well as the piazza above was illuminated by large reflecting lamps, when on such occasions congregated the ladies and gentlemen who were stopping there either permanently or merely temporarily to while away the time and watch the life and bustle on the road in front of the Inn, as well as in the yard beyond; the shouts and activity of the hostlers and stablemen at the arrival or departure of the mail or post coach, the rapidity with which the horses were unhitched, or replaced by fresh relays after the passengers had refreshed themselves, the number of travelers on horseback or private conveyance, the occasional toot of a stage horn or ringing of the hostler's bell, all tended to form a continuous change of scene. In 1823 there were no less than eleven principal lines of "Land Stages," daily running on the turnpike to and from Philadelphia past the Eagle. These were known as the "Berwick," "Downingtown," "Harrisburg Coachee," "Harrisburg Stage," "Lancaster Accommodation," "Lancaster Coachee," "Lancaster and Pittsburg Mail," "Mifflin, Lewistown, via Harrisburg," "Philadelphia and Pittsburg via York," "Pittsburg via Harrisburg," "Philadelphia and West Chester" besides numerour lines of accommodation stages. The fare for way passengers was usually six cents per mile; through fare from Philadelphia to Pittsburg was $18.50 each way, meals and lodging extra.

The "Coachee" was a carriage peculiar to America, the body was rather longer than that of a coach, but of the same shape. In the front it was left open down to the bottom, and the driver sat on a bench under the roof of the carriage. There were two seats in it for passengers, who sat with their faces towards the horses. The roof was supported by posts placed at the corners, on each side of the doors, above the panels; it was open and to guard

THE WAYSIDE INNS ON THE LANCASTER ROAD.

OLD INNS ON THE LANCASTER TURNPIKE.

NOT IDENTIFIED.
THE SHIP TAVERN (No. 31) NEAR 27TH MILESTONE.

NOT IDENTIFIED.
MOUNT VERNON (No. 48) BETWEEN 45TH AND 46TH MILESTONE.

against bad weather; there were curtains made to let down from the roof and fasten to buttons placed for the purpose on the outside. There was also a leathern curtain to hang occasionally between the driver and the passengers. The Coachee had doors at the side, since the panels and body were generally finely finished and varnished.

As an instance of the importance of the Spread Eagle as a post town, a comparison of the receipts of the United States post office for the year ending March 31, 1827, shows there was a larger amount of postage collection there than at any other tavern post office on the turnpike east of Downingtown, viz.: $60.25. During the same period the collections at the Paoli were but $6.54.

In the year 1825, Edward W. Siter became the landlord of the Spread Eagle and remained until 1836, when Stephen Horne appears as the lessee, who had for some time been connected with the house.

On the evening of September 15th, 1834, an incident occurred which probably caused more excitement and sensation in the immediate vicinity of Siterville than had ever been known on any previous occasion within the memory of the oldest inhabitant. This was caused by the descent of Mr. James Mills' balloon, which had started on an aerial voyage from Philadelphia at half-past four o'clock in the afternoon. The following is the bold aeronaut's own description of what took place:

"Warned by the increasing obscurity of the world below I began to descend and at six o'clock and twenty minutes reached the earth in a fine green field, near the Spread Eagle, on the Lancaster Turnpike, 16 miles from Philadelphia. As I descended very slowly, two young gentlemen and Dr. M——, of Philadelphia, came to my assistance, and laying hold of the car in which I remained towed

me about a quarter of a mile to the tavern, where I
alighted, balloon and passenger, safe and sound. Before
discharging the gas, several ladies got successively into the
car and were let up as far as the anchor rope would permit.
The gas was let out and the balloon folded.   In doing this
a cricket was unfortunately included, and having to cut his
way out he made the only break in the balloon which occurred on this expedition.   Mr. Horne, of the Spread
Eagle, treated me with great kindness, and Dr. M——
politely offered me a conveyance to the city, which I
reached at one o'clock this morning."

After the completion of the railroad which was located
at this point, about half a mile to the north of the turnpike,
and the successful attempt at steam transportation, the
decline of the Inn was rapid, the glory of the once noted
hostelry waned year after year, and it soon became merely
a cross road country tavern with no patronage except what
the laboring population in the vicinity supplied.

The only exception to this desolation was during the
winter when the sleighing was good then for a time the
old tavern would for a short period be galvanized into a
new life as it were.   Open house would be held all night;
four to six musicians were in attendance, and as sleigh load
after sleigh load of young people would arrive to refresh
themselves and enjoy a dance or two, some of the old
scenes of life and activity approximating the former glories
of the tavern were reproduced.   To such as participated
in any of these parties the cheerful rubicund face of the
host will no doubt be recalled, whether it was Ned Siter,
Steve Horn, or Benny Kirk.   However even these sleighing parties are now things of the past, and almost unknown
to the present generation in the vicinity.

After changing ownership many times the Inn finally

came into possession of George W. Childs, of Philadelphia, who bought the property so as to prevent anyone obtaining a license for the sale of liquor so near his venture at Wayne station, a short distance below on the turnpike.

In the following Summer the use of the building was given by its benevolent owner to the Managers of the Lincoln Institution of Philadelphia as a Summer home for the large number of Indian girls who were being trained and educated by that Institution. Fears had been entertained by the Managers and patrons of the Institution that a hot Summer in the city might prove disastrous to the Indian children, so it was determined to try the experiment of sending the girls to the country for half the year provided such removal would in no way interfere with their training or studies. Therefore the Managers of the school concluded to accept the kind and opportune offer of Mr. Childs allowing them the use of the old Inn and surrounding grounds free of charge. It, however, cost the Institution over a thousand dollars to make the former hostelry habitable and suitable for their purpose. It was not long before almost a hundred girls were so established in their new temporary home and the experiment from the very start proved itself a complete success.

The old Spread Eagle once more became a point of attraction, not only with the residents or sojourners in the vicinity, but also for the curious and sympathetic, some from a remote distance. Public religious services were held every Sunday at Wayne Hall; these services were always largely attended, on which occasion the choir, music and the responses, according to the ritual of the Protestant Episcopal Church, were entirely rendered by the Indian girls, who seemed to thoroughly comprehend the meaning of the services.

It was a beautiful, yet strange spectacle to see these dusky maidens, descendants of the aborigines, going two by two, from their services, as they trudged along the smooth white turnpike, sober and demure with their prayer book and hymnal in their hands; where but a little over two centuries ago their people had roamed and hunted free and undisturbed by anything approaching civilization, as monarchs of these glorious hills and valleys. Now no vestige of this former race remains but an occasional arrow dart ploughed up by the husbandman as he tills the soil. During these two summers several traveling Indian bands that visited Philadelphia also visited the school at the old Inn, and it is said that the impressions made upon their minds, and the reports they made when they returned home were of the greatest use to the school. Probably the most noteworthy and interesting of the visits was the one when the celebrated "Sitting Bull" accompanied by his band, all resplendent in scarlet blankets, leggings and feathers, with faces and hands daubed and streaked with vermilion and chrome yellow, came and spent a few hours at the old inn; quite a feast was prepared for them by the Indian girls which they seemed to enjoy, still not a muscle moved in their stolid countenances which could be construed as either showing approbation or displeasure.

One of the most interesting events during the sojourn of the Indian girls at the old tavern was the entertainment given on the evening of September 24, 1884, at Wayne Hall. It consisted of a series of twenty-two tableaux illustrative of Longfellow's beautiful poem of Hiawatha. The Rev. Joseph L. Miller, chaplain of the institution, read those portions of the poem descriptive of the scenes as presented by the dusky children. There were 10 characters represented in the tableaux. All the scenes passed

THE WAYSIDE INNS ON THE LANCASTER ROAD.

GALLAGHERVILLE.
REAR VIEW OF THE "GENERAL WAYNE."

GALLAGHERVILLE TAVERN (No. 35), NEAR 33D MILESTONE.
THE "GENERAL WAYNE" (No. 28), NEAR 22D MILESTONE.

PHOTOS. BY JULIUS F. SACHSE, 1886.

off successfully, and were well applauded by the large audience present. Among the most vivid pictures were "The Indian's Home," Hiawatha's "infancy" with an Indian Lullaby, and "Hunting," "The Ambush," "Hunters' Return" and "Lover's Advent." The "Wedding Feast," with its songs and dances were the crowning features of the evening. In this scene the stage was filled with the girls and boys of the institution all in striking costumes brilliant in color and beads, feathers, tassels, fringes and other trinkets. A wedding song was sung, then came the dance, after which a chorus of over thirty Indians sang a hymn in the Dakota language.

The old tavern was used by the Lincoln Institution during the years 1884–5, when after several vain attempts on part of the managers to buy the property from Mr. Childs, they vacated the old Inn and purchased ten acres of woodland on the northern slope of the south Valley hill, about 1 ½ miles northeast of the old inn, where they erected three large buildings as a permanent summer school; this is now known as "Po-ne-mah."

The suburban village and improvements which have sprung up on all sides of the old hostelry, with the attendant pleasure travel, on the turnpike now again put in first class condition by the Lancaster Avenue Impovement Company, so far have had little effect on old "Siterville." At the present writing (1886) the old inn though in good repair is closed and without an occupant, and looms up on the roadside like a dark and sombre relic of the past, with nothing to remind the present generation of its departed glories.

THE WARREN TAVERN NEAR THE 20TH MILE STONE.

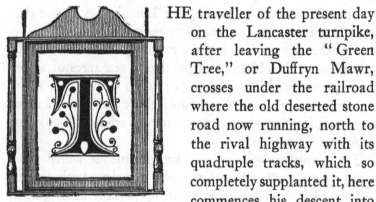

HE traveller of the present day on the Lancaster turnpike, after leaving the "Green Tree," or Duffryn Mawr, crosses under the railroad where the old deserted stone road now running, north to the rival highway with its quadruple tracks, which so completely supplanted it, here commences his descent into the Great Chester Valley, winding around the hillside. After passing the Green Tree store, so long presided over by the Bakers and Philips, and the new hall of Thomson Lodge, No. 340, F. & A. M., the twentieth mile stone with the attendant toll-booth, is soon reached. At this point the pike enters a gorge in the chain of the South Valley hills, and at the foot, after crossing the long stone bridge over the rivulet which pours down the hillside through the ravine which here intersects the

PHOTOS, BY JULIUS F. SACHSE. 1899

THE WARREN TAVERN (No. 27), NEAR 20TH MILESTONE.

THE WARREN SHOPS.
RUINS OF BARN.

RESTING PLACE OF THE FAHNESTOCKS.
THE WARREN TAVERN IN 1886.

a commodious house, of ample dimensions, two stories in height, capped by a sharp gable, pierced with three dormer windows, the enclosure within the bounds of the snow-white picket fence (1888) dotted with numerous outbuildings—the evergreens of stately growth, all tend to attract the attention of the traveller of the present day, and give the stranger an impression that the structure is one of more than ordinary importance, and a well-preserved relic of a former period—perhaps dating back to the Colonial period, and that it was the home of some brave, sturdy soldier of the Revolution, who wore the blue and buff, and on many a field performed deeds of valor and prowess while opposing the hireling invader.

In the first surmise the stranger would be correct. The house in question, and the more primitive structure which it replaced, was for over a century one of the best known landmarks on the Lancaster roadside. When first opened as a public house in the fourth decade of the last century, the sign-board as it swung and creaked in the wind bore the image and name of Admiral Vernon. This was, however, soon changed to the Admiral Warren. After the Revolution, in turnpike days, it was known to all travellers as the "Warren," the British Admiral giving place on the sign-board to the patriot general, who died for his country on Bunker Hill. After the turnpike was completed toward the close of last century, it was not long before the house became a tavern stand or stage house of the first class, being equaled in reputation and patronage only by the "Eagle," "Paoli" and "Downings"; the reputation of the "Good-cheer" and the cleanliness of the bedding made it one of the most desirable stopping places on the thoroughfare. Among the guests who patronized the inn, and

4

who found shelter under the hospitable rooftree, drank the wines, and enjoyed the products of the larder, were to be numbered presidents, judges, foreign potentates, and the most distinguished travelers from this and foreign climes.

The scenes of life and activity then to be seen daily in the "tavern yard" in front of the hostelry were not surpassed at any other point on the road; the arrival and departure of the stagecoaches, the genial host "Funnystock" always present to greet the new arrivals, or to wish the departing ones bon voyage; the bustling hostlers and stablemen, together with the shouts of the drovers, busy in the large cattle pens, stables and shelters, then on the opposite side of the turnpike, the passing teamsters, with strings of tinkling bells on the horse yokes, all tended to make up the ever-recurring scenes of excitement at this renowned halting place on the Lancaster roadside.

When, however, in the course of time the stone age of travel, as the turnpike days may well be called, was superseded by that of iron and steam, the Warren, in common with its chief competitor the "Spread-Eagle," was left stranded far from the new road, and soon the inn from being one of the most busy spots between Philadelphia and Lancaster rapidly fell into decay, and after the withdrawal of the stagecoaches dropped to the level of an ordinary cross-road country tavern, and at the present day all that is left to remind the present generation of even the existence of such a noted landmark is the name of the local postoffice, viz.: "Warren Tavern," and even this is in danger of being before long a thing of the past, as lately there has been started a movement looking to a change of name, as was the case with the "Spread-Eagle" by some supercilious newcomers, on whose sensitive ears the word

THE WAYSIDE INNS ON THE LANCASTER ROAD.

PHOTOS. BY JULIUS F. SACHSE, 1896.

"HALFWAY" HOUSE, DOWNINGTOWN (No. 33),
NEAR 31st MILESTONE.
SWAN TAVERN, DOWNINGTOWN (No. 34),
NEAR 31st MILESTONE.

THE "SHEAF OF WHEAT" (No. 30),
NEAR 26th MILESTONE.
ORIGINAL "SHIP" TAVERN (No. 36),
NEAR 32d MILESTONE.

"Tavern" seems to grate harshly, and who have no idea of the derivation of the name, and who if they achieve their object may perhaps succeed in replacing the name of the revolutionary hero with that of one of his British of Hessian opponents, a proceeding which would be entirely in keeping with the course pursued by the Anglo-maniacs who have lately cropped out among us.

How in 1733 the great road from Lancaster was laid out to a point in Chester County, near the "Sign of the White Horse," and the action taken by the residents of Tredyffrin, Easttown and Willistown and adjoining townships to have the road completed to the Schuylkill has been set forth in the preceding articles. It was not until November 6, 1741, when the final return of the commissioners giving the route to the Schuylkill was presented to Lieut. Governor George Thomas and Council. By this report we find that the new road was laid out eastward from the "Sign of the White Horse" along the old road "until near Robert Powell's House, then leaving the old road, and on George Aston's land south 72 degrees, east 200 perches to a run, thence 80 perches, whence it again meets the old road, then on it south 33½ degrees, east 21 perches, then in Willistown south 33½ degrees, 20 perches, &c., &c."

By the above survey it will be seen that at the time there was no house on the site of the Warren, or mention would certainly have been made of it. It is safe to assume that George Aston built the house as soon as the road was open for travel, at the point where the road crossed the run, and the ascent of Valley Hill commenced through the notch, or gulf before described. This was not until 1743–4, and in the latter year we find Aston a resident of East Whiteland, as well as a prominent member of St. Peter's congregation in the Valley. He was also an active factor

in building the stone church (St. Peter's) in the Valley.
The church records state that: "April 15th, 1745, was
held a vestry in St. Peter's Church, which was the first
there ever held." George Aston is among those chosen as
vestrymen, and in the subsequent allotment of pews No. 4
fell to his lot. He was the eldest son of George Aston,
who purchased 500 acres of land, and settled in Caln. He
was a prominent citizen, and served as one of the justices
of the county from 1724 to 1729. In the administration
of his office he, however, seems to have been too zealous
by encouraging litigation where it should have been
avoided. Complaint of this fact being made, and coming
to the knowledge of Hon. Patrick Gordon, the Governor
acquainted the board that it was necessary that a new commission of "the Peace for Chester county should be issue,
and that he had some very good reasons for leaving out
one, viz : George Aston, who had acted but too much, &c."

George Aston, the elder, died in 1738, leaving two sons
and three daughters. George, the eldest, and builder of
the old wayside inn, married a daughter of Owen Thomas,
of East Whiteland, and became the owner of the property
now known as the Warren property. Application for
license was no doubt made to the Court as soon as the
house was ready for occupancy. This was granted in
1745. The inn was located, as was then the universal custom, near or at a running stream of water, and situated
about midway between its rivals—the "Blue Ball" and
the "Sign of the White Horse"—became from the start
the stopping place for the churchmen and missionaries as
they journeyed along the road. The house when first
licensed was named the "Admr. Vernon," after a celebrated British naval officer, Sir Edward Vernon, the hero
of Porto Bello, and who in view of his achievements was

then the idol of England. With the outbreak of the French and Indian troubles, the gallant capture of Louisburg, June 17, 1745, followed by the victories over the French fleet in 1747 by Admiral Peter Warren, K.C.B., the latter soon became the ideal hero of the war party in the province, of which Aston was a prominent member; and it was not long before the former hero was supplanted in the minds of the people by the latter, whose deeds of valor were performed really to protect the colonies.

The change on the sign board of our wayside inn was probably made in 1748 when Aston relinquished the house to one Daniel Goldsmith, who rented the inn. It appears from the records that for some reason, not stated, the new host was refused a license by the Governor in the next year, 1749. George Aston then again took charge, but when the French and Indian troubles broke out in 1753, threatening the lives and homes of the inhabitants of the Chester Valley, while the Governor and the council were squabbling as to whether there should be any defence or not, George Aston was among the first men in the county to form a company for the defence of the province, and with them did his duty well in checking the infuriated savages in Northampton County.

In the account of the public expenditures of the day we find an entry, March 2, 1756, where the Assembly voted £240, 15s. 4d. " to Captain George Aston for himself and his companys pay."

On account of Captain Aston's prominence as a military man, the house now became a rendezvous and center for the military as well as the church party in this section of the county. In most of the local military documents from

Braddock to Stanwix we find "George Aston's" noted as a landmark and stopping place. Aston's son, Owen, became the County "Wagon Master," while in Roger Hunt's account book of 1759, who was a brother-in-law of Captain Aston's, we find frequent reference to "George Aston at ye Admiral Warren."

Aston appears to have kept the house during these troublesome times, when the French and Indians inspired so much fear in the community, until 1760, when he was succeeded as host by one Peter Valleau. Three years later Aston and his wife sold the property to Lynford Lardner, of Philadelphia, a brother-in-law of Richard Penn, and who was the agent of the Penn family in America. Valleau continued until 1767. Nothing of note is known to have occurred during his occupancy.

He was succeeded by Caleb Parry, who deserves more than a passing notice. He was the son of David Parry, of Tredyffrin, whose father, James Parry, donated the ground on which the Great Valley Presbyterian Church was built. During the French and Indian times David Parry was one of the associators, and the lad, Caleb, no doubt imbibed much of his military spirit from him, and at the very outbreak of the Revolution we find Caleb Parry commissioned as Lieutenant Colonel in Colonel Atlee's "First Regiment of Pennsylvany Musketry," recruited mainly from among the Presbyterians in the Chester and Pequea Valleys. He was active in all the military operations around New York, which culminated so disastrously to the patriot cause, and on the memorable 27th of August, 1776, in the engagement known as the Battle of Long Island, Colonel Parry was numbered among the slain, as his brother officers stated, "Dying like a hero." An account of the affair states:

THE "CROSS KEYS" (HAND'S PASS), (No. 39),
NEAR 38TH MILESTONE.
THE "STATE ARMS" (No. 43), NEAR 40TH
MILESTONE.

"SADSBURY" (BAER'S OR KINDIG'S), (No. 44),
NEAR 41ST MILESTONE.
THE "RAINBOW" (No. 40), BETWEEN 88TH AND 89TH
MILESTONE.

"The men shrunk and fell back, but Atlee rallied them and Parry cheered them on and they gained the hill. It was here, while engaged in an officer's highest duty, turning men to the enemy by his own example, that the fatal bullet pierced his brow."

To return to the roadside inn during the second year that Parry was in charge, a danger threatened the inn. This was nothing more or less than the petition for license of a new house between the Warren and the Blue Ball. Parry fearing this would injure his business appealed to his landlord, Lynford Lardner, to use his influence with the Governor to prevent a license being granted to Joshua Evans, the new applicant. Lardner in pursuance to the request sent a protest to the Court, in which he states that about six years before he had purchased the estate of George Aston and wife, three and a half miles from "Blue Ball" and three miles from "White Horse," and he feared the establishment of another tavern between his and the Blue Ball would discourage his tenant, &c. The protest, however, did not avail, as the license was granted and the "General Paoli" was the result. Parry remained at the Warren for another year after the Paoli was opened, when he resigned in favor of Isaac Webb, who was there 1771–2–3. He was also a renter and was followed by Samuel Johnson, in 1774. In this year Lynford Lardner, the owner of the property, died October 6th, and his will, proved October 25, 1774, following curious provision is made. He orders that his executors "do sell and dispose of the iron works newly erected, known as the Andover Iron Works, in the Province of New Jersey, and also my messuage and tenniment, commonly called by the name of Warren Tavern, in the county of Chester, and the plantations and lands thereunto belonging, which I purchased

from George Asheton and wife, for the payment of just
debts, and for other purposes in this, my last will, &c., &c."

In pursuance with the above provision, Catharine Lardner and John Lardner, the executors, November 2, 1776,
conveyed the "Admiral Warren plantation, in Whiteland
township," to Hon. John Penn, of Philadelphia.

Samuel Johnson was the tenant until the property was
transferred to the new owner, when he was succeeded by
Peter Mather, a man of strong Tory proclivities.

During the term of Webb and Johnson the old inn seems
to have lost prestige. This was partially caused by the
"General Paoli" becoming the favorite gathering place of
the patriot spirits, with which the locality abounded,
while the Warren and the Unicorn, seven miles below, had
the reputation of being loyal houses.

Local tradition tells us that the Warren became the
gathering place for the Tories in the vicinity, and such
persons as were disaffected to the patriot cause. Further
that after the outbreak of active hostilities, meetings were
frequently held in the house, where British envoys, or officers, were present, and information which had been obtained was sent to the enemy. Notable among the visitors
to the inn at the time was the talented, but unfortunate,
Major Andre, who was then a paroled prisoner of war at
Lancaster, and who had the liberty of certain roads, among
which was the Philadelphia road to within a point twenty
miles from the city.

What good use Andre made of his parole may be surmised, when it is known that he is said to have mapped
the country and suggested the capture of Philadelphia by
way of the Chesapeake and Great Valley, the plan so successfully carried out by Howe and Cornwallis in the Fall
of 1777.

In the year 1777, when it was destined that the tide of war should surge through our fertile valley—then the garden of Pennsylvania—the house was in charge of Peter Mather, who, if our traditions be true, was like his predecessor, a strong tory. This is further strengthened by the fact that when the British Army was quartered in the valley Mather was one of the few who appears to have suffered no loss, while his immediate neighbors lost almost all of their possessions.

On the eventful night of the 20th of September, when the cohorts of the enemy under Grey, accompanied by his aid, Major Andre, silently marched up the Swedeford road, they wheeled to the left at the road which led to the Warren, where a halt was made, and to divert suspicion from the real traitors who guided the advance, the patriotic blacksmith at the shops, then situated on the south side of the old Lancaster road just north of the present turnpike bridge, was forced to get out of his bed and accompany the column. This dreadful occurrence of this dark night it is unnecessary to repeat here, as they are well-known in history as the "Massacre at Paoli," and have been graphically described by more able pens than that of the writer.

After the British had left the vicinity Mather, the inn keeper, was publicly charged by his neighbors as being responsible for the massacre, also of having guided the British. Both of these accusations he strenuously denied, producing proof that he had not been out of the house during the night. In confirmation of his statements are the two facts, viz.: First, that in no known British letter, report or account is mention made of Peter Mather, or his connection with the attack; second, that notwithstanding the suspicion attached to him he was permitted to continue to live in the house and keep the inn for a number of years. The

place, however, was shunned and avoided by most of the
residents of the vicinity, and the inn keeper drew his patronage from the chance travellers on the road, who knew nothing of the odium common report attached to the unfortunate Boniface. From these facts it may be surmised that
the enterprise was not a financial success.

About the close of the Revolutionary war there was considerable excitement throughout the county in reference to
the proposed removal of the county seat from Chester, on
the Delaware, to a more central part in the county. There
were three points suggested, all being public houses, viz.:
"Downing's," the "Turk's Head" (now West Chester),
and the "Admiral Warren," with the chances in favor of
the latter on account of its position in the Great Valley,
and being within easy reach from all points in the county;
but the fact that the property was owned by one of the
Penn family, together with the state of the popular feeling
towards anything which savored of the old régime, precluded the acceptance of the locality on any condition.
Notwithstanding the activity of John Penn's agents and
friends the agitation of the matter only tended the more to
incense the populace against the old inn; consequently,
when in 1783, the Assembly passed an Act (March 19)
doubling the rates of all tavern licenses, the outlook became still darker for Mather. He, however, held out
until the property was sold, when he made a sale of his
personal effects and went to West Chester. Shortly after
the removal of the county seat there he kept a licensed
house within the new borough, again succeeding, it is said,
the very man—Isaac Webb—who had occupied the "Warren" prior to Mather. In the new location his expectations again failed to be realized, so after remaining for a
year or two he seems to have drifted to the city, where his

THE WAYSIDE INNS ON THE LANCASTER ROAD.

THE LANCASTER TURNPIKE AT 43D MILESTONE—"OLD MOSCOW."

MANTUA ACADEMY NEAR 43D MILESTONE.   THE "GENERAL WAYNE" (NO. 46) AT 43D MILESTONE.

THE "GENERAL WAYNE" FROM SOUTHWEST.

ill fortune followed him; as the people who knew him were
wont to say "God frowned on him," so he fell lower and
lower in the social scale. First he drove team or dray,
but finally in his old age came down to pushing a hand
cart or wheelbarrow, and even here the boys were wont to
make his existence miserable by calling after him "Here
we are and there we go," and " Remember Paoli."

The ownership of the old Roadside Inn now passed into
the possession of the Fahnestock family, in whose hands it
was to remain for more than half a century, and reach a
renown and popularity second to none of the sixty odd
hostelries on the roadside between the city and Lancaster.

Many are the tales told of how Fahnestock bought the
house; how the vendue crier refused his bid on account of
his uncouth appearance as he stood there in his long coat
of undyed homespun, secured by large hooks and eyes in
lieu of buttons; his long straggling beard and hair but
partly hidden by his broad brimmed hat, his homemade
cowhide boots, and worse than all he was clad in a pair of
pantaloons, a fact which made him the butt of all present.
Then how he produced the bright jingling coin, and told
the crier that if his bids wouldn't count his money would,
and the subsequent discomfiture of the vendue crier. These
tales and many more of a similar import were told and
retold in the barrooms, and to travelers in stages along the
road until they were as current on the pike as they were
among the children of the cross-roads school, or among the
old crones who sat besides the hearth, "A whirling their
wheel, or quilting the coverlids."

The true facts of the case are that John Penn, the owner
of the property, was anxious to dispose of the whole property. This by some means became known to Casper Fahnestock, a member of the German Mystic Community at

Ephrata, and resulted in Casper, accompanied by Brother
Jabez (Rev. Peter Miller), the prior of the congregation,
and another brother, making a pilgrimage down the Lancaster road in the last week of March, 1786, to Philadelphia. They traveled on foot, as was their custom, clad in
the rough habit of their order with staff in hand, Casper,
in addition, carrying a pair of saddle bags. When the trio
arrived at the Warren they craved admittance, but received
a rebuff from Mather, who told them "no beggars were
wanted around there," so the three brethren continued on
to the city. Penn, who was known to Brother Jabez, was
at once called on, the price agreed upon, the conveyance
made, executed and acknowledged in open court, March
31, 1786, before Hon. Edward Shippen, President-Judge
of the Common pleas. This document states that the
Hon. John Penn, Esquire, and Dame Anne, his wife, con-
vey to Casper Fahnestock, of Cocalico township, Lancaster
county, shopkeeper, the Warren Tavern plantation of 337
acres, the consideration being two thousand pounds lawful
money of Pennsylvania in specie of gold or silver. This
money was paid out of the saddlebags which Casper had
carried all the way from Ephrata, the subscribing witnesses
being Peter Miller and Joan Louis Patey. The trio immediately started west on their return in the same manner as
they had come. Casper's saddlebags were lightened of
their weight of coin, but contained the plantation in its
stead. On their arrival at the tavern, it was long after
nightfall. The mystic brethren, however, stopped and
inquired for Mather, who had, it seems, already gone to
bed. As the latter came down in gown and slippers, Casper told him that he was now the owner of the property,
and intended to remain and examine his purchase in the
morning, a proceeding to which there was no objection

from the now obsequious Mather. In a few days the old Tory made a vendue, at which Casper was a frequent bidder, and ere the first week of April had elapsed the old Roadside Inn was in charge of the German Sabbatarian from the Monastery on the Cocalico. The new host, although an old man, being over sixty years of age, soon made his presence felt with the wagoners and travellers on the road. In view of the succeeding events, an extended notice of the first of the name in Chester county, as well as his successors will not be amiss.

Casper Fahnestock was a native of Germany, born in 1724. He was the eldest son of Dietrich Fahnestock, the founder of the "whole tribe of Fahnestocks" (in America), as the inscription calls him on his tombstone in the old God's Acre of the Sabbath-keepers at Ephrata, on the banks of the Cocalico. Dietrich, the elder, came to this country with his wife, child and two sisters, in 1726. His sole possessions consisted of an axe, a weaver's shuttle, a Bible and a German thaler. He first settled on the Raritan River in New Jersey where the family lived for a number of years, but becoming convinced of the truth of the Sabbatarian doctrine, joined that body of Christians, and about 1748 we find the family residents of Ephrata. In the next year, June 21, 1749, a patent was granted him by the Governor for 329 acres of land at ? ? ? ? as the founder of the "Chester County" Fahnestocks. Casper, as were the rest of the family, was a member of the Ephrata community; his aunt even entered the Convent Saron, and became known as "Sister Armilla"; they were all consistent Sabbath-keepers, Casper and his wife Maria in addition keeping several other mosaic laws, such as eschewing the use of pork, the use of meats and milk at the same meals, &c. It was from these peculiarities that the common impression arose among his English neighbors, that the family were of the Jewish faith.

The new owner had no sooner taken charge than the tavern at once became the stopping place for all of the Lancaster county Germans. Menish, Dunker, Omish, Lutheran, Reformist and Moravian all found shelter and entertainment with the old "Sieben-Tager"* from Ephrata. Casper was ably seconded by the members of his family; his wife Maria, and mother-in-law, Elizabeth Gleim, took charge of the kitchen, the oldest son Charles presided over the bar, Daniel, who was a cripple, and his brother Dietrich, assisted in the house and tavern-yard, while the two other children, Esther and Catherine, with Charles' wife Susan, attended to the wants of the house, table and guests. Just six months after the family were domiciled in the old tavern Casper's wife's mother, Elizabeth Gleim, died in her 75th year. She was buried on the plantation in a small clearing on the northern slope of South Valley Hill, about one fourth of a mile from the tavern, according to the custom of the Sabbatarians of that day; due north and south, with prayer and song, the ceremonies being conducted by the reverend Prior, of the Ephrata community, Brother Jabez. This spot was in the course of time surrounded by a low stone wall and became the burial ground of the Fahnestock family (Chester county branch) and now through neglect and the ravages of time has become about as gruesome a place of sepulture as it is possible to imagine.

At this period of history the German element had increased to so great an extent in our State, that it actually became a question whether the State should not become a German State, and that all judicial and legislative proceed-

* Member of the mystic Seventh-day Baptist Community of Ephrata, Lancaster Co., Penna.

THE WAYSIDE INNS ON THE LANCASTER ROAD.

OLD INNS ON THE LANCASTER TURNPIKE.

NOT IDENTIFIED.
MT. VERNON (No. 48) FROM WEST.

PHOTO. BY OWEN M. BRUNER, ESQ., 1912.

NOT IDENTIFIED.
WASHINGTON TAVERN (No. 42) WEST OF 42D MILESTONE.

ings be held in that language. In 1787, the German high school was established with a grant of 10,000 acres of land. German was introduced into the different charity and township schools; all tending to lay the foundation for a German commonwealth; the plan cherished by the projectors was to eradicate the English language completely. The German element held together and won victory after victory at the polls over the "*die dummen Irischer,*" as their English-speaking opponents were called. At last their preponderance became so great that everything seemed favorable to bring about the result, viz.: That the German language would be legally declared to be the tongue of the commonwealth, when the French revolution broke out with its attendant influx of French refugees, French ideas of atheism, (foreign to the German character), liberty, equality, etc., etc. This was followed by the general war in Europe, and the almost total cessation of emigration from Germany. During this state of affairs the English-speaking element gained strength from day to day, and the German struggle for supremacy, so auspiciously begun, soon declined; and it was not long before the high school at Lancaster, which was to have been the great university of America, became a thing of the past. Politically, however, the Germans for many years continued to hold the balance of power.

Among the wagoners and travelers on the turnpike the German element was so largely in the majority that no public house could succeed unless some one in charge was conversant with the German tongue. As there was no question about the nationality of the new host of the Warren, he being German to the core, his great difficulty was from the start to provide for those who sought his shelter. Further, by his attention to business and the cleanliness of the house, the Inn soon became a desirable stopping place for "Irisher" or "Gentleman," as well as for the "Deutscher." It even became a station for the professional express rider, a character and occupation long since passed away and forgotten.

Thus matters went on, the patronage and renown of "the Dutch tavern," as it was called by the wagoners, increased with the travel of the road, and the proprietor kept pace with the requirements of the traveling public. Casper kept the Corduroy Causeway through the swamp in better repair than it had been heretofore, a proceeding which pleased the frequenters of the road and proved another feature to attract custom to the Inn. This causeway was to the north of the present turnpike bridge, and before this time was one of the worst places on the Lancaster road, being often impassable in the spring and winter.

Some idea of the difficulties of the travel in that day may be gleaned from the following letters, written just a century ago by Miss Marie Penry, the daughter of a celebrated Welsh physician. She was one of the Moravian Sisterhood at Lititz, and gives a graphic description of her trip from Philadelphia to Lancaster. Nothing could illustrate more forcibly the great change which has taken place during the century in the time and manner of communication between the two places. Miss Penry writes that she set out from Philadelphia on a Friday morning in November, leaving the city at 8 o'clock. Her traveling companions consisted besides the driver of Mr. Tilt and wife, and two children, seven years old, twins. He was a British officer who had been a prisoner of war at Lancaster, and there married, and on his release went to Halifax, and was now on his way to see his relatives. This composed the load. When they arrived at Fahnestock's they stopped for refreshment for man and beast, and there met an Irish gentleman and his wife who had arrived in the country but a few days before, and were now on their way to the western end of the county. They had hired a chair and came thus far, when their driver refused to proceed on account of the bad condition of the roads, and being unable to procure any conveyance were in consequence stranded in a strange land. When the party started on their journey they took the "Irish Gentlewoman" as the letter calls her, in the stage with them, and as her husband could not even get a horse for hire, he was obliged to travel on foot along side of the stage. Thus the journey to the Brandywine commenced. It was, however, not destined to continue to the end of their goal, as the extra weight in the stage with the roughness of the road, had a bad effect on the vehicle, which proved unequal to the strain. The party had not proceeded far ere a crack was heard, and the hind axle broke, letting the stage down on the road. Fortunately the horses were stopped and the passengers gotten out of the wreck without injury. The party, the letter continues, now all footed it Indian fashion to the nearest inn, which was about two miles from where the stage broke down (probably the Sheaf of Wheat). On their arrival they partook of an ordinary wayside meal. The spirits of the party were clouded by the prospect of having to pass Saturday and perhaps Sunday there. However, after the meal was finished a countryman offered to take the party to Downing's for a consideration, as a great favor. His team proved to be a country wagon without springs or cover, with no seats other than bundles of rye straw. Into this vehicle, Miss Penry continues, we went with all our packages, and our Irish gentleman, who seemed to think that "humble riding was better than proud walking on

5

foot" was but too glad to avail himself of the opportunity to join the party. Thus the party arrived long after dark at the hospitable house of the "Downings"; as the fair writer adds—"Politeness and good nature had lessened every difficulty."

The time, 1789, from Philadelphia to Downings, was over twelve hours, express time 1889 is one hour.

At this period there were two matters agitating the community, both of which seriously affected the usually imperturbable inn-keeper. One was the question of making a stone highway, chaussie, or turnpike, to take the place of the old road. The second was the action taken by the Federal government in taxing whiskey, a matter which was destined to lead to the most serious consequences.

A fact not generally known is, that the first organized opposition to the new excise law, took place in our Chester county, and the exciseman or collector was roughly used, barely escaping with his life. The rioters, however, were convicted and punished severely by the State Courts. On that occasion the foreman of the jury told the Attorney General "that he was much or more opposed to the excise law than the rioters, but would not suffer violators of the law to go unpunished."

This opposition thus started extended to the western counties, where it culminated in 1794, in what is known in history as the "Whiskey insurrection." When President Washington issued his requisition for military force to quell the incipient insurrection against Federal authority, Governor Mifflin, in response to the Federal proclamation, made a personal tour through the eastern part of the State to arouse the military spirit of the populace. In the progress of this trip he came through Chester county and addressed the people at various points, among others the

Warren Tavern is named, where, it is stated that, notwithstanding the protests from the proprietor, who, as a consistent Sabbath-keeper, was a non-combatant, a recruiting office was opened and a company recruited by Edward Pearce, which became known as "Captain Parker's Company" of Colonel Harris' Regiment, Edward Pearce being promoted to the Adjutancy. It was not long before the tocsin of war, the piercing note of the fife, and the heavy tread of armed men was again heard in our peaceful valley. Most of the troops, however, marched by way of the Swedesford, striking the Lancaster road a little below the "White Horse." The baggage and supplies came out over the new turnpike, which had been made here and there in sections between the Warren and the city, but which on account of the ignorance displayed by those having the enterprise in charge was almost impassable, even for the baggage trains. However, the incipient war in Western Pennsylvania was soon over, when the efforts to perfect the new turnpike were redoubled; the long bridge was built and the new road at the "Warren" occupied almost all the roadbed of the provincial thoroughfare. Casper, to be up to the times, and foreseeing the large increase in the travel, at an early day set about to prepare materials for a new house on as large a scale as the Siters had built six miles below. This new house was built so as to face on the north side of the turnpike. The old "Admiral Vernon," similar to all of the inns on the Lancaster road, was built on the south side of the road, and it was not long ere the new sign board of the "General Warren" swung in its yoke on a high mast near the southeast angle of the new turnpike tavern.

With the native thrift of old Casper and his family all the work had to be done by themselves—trees were felled, hewed and sawed, lime burned, sand hauled and stone quarried—for the new hostelry. A curious anecdote is told about old Casper in connection with the latter labor: During the fine moonlight nights in summer "Old Cas," as he was called, would make his men work in the quarry long after supper, or, at least, would go and swing the sledge by himself. This was not to the taste of the young generation, and several made up their minds that they would stop the old German and get him out of his Dutch notions. So the Pearce boys, the next night, rigged themselves up in horns and blankets, carrying heavy log chains, and quietly getting near where the old man was cracking the stone in the moonlight, jumped up, rattled their chains and uttered unearthly yells. The old man, startled for a moment, resumed his labor as unconcerned as if they were trees, merely saying: "I bees not afrait von yous if you bees der teufel," finishing up with, "Wer auf Gott vertraut kan weder tod nocht teufel schaden,"* and calmly continued his work.

Another one relates how it would worry the old man during harvest when the mowers or reapers would sit down longer for rest or refreshments than he thought they ought to, and when he could stand it no longer he would come up and say, "Now, poys, youse takes a bissel grog (whiskey and water) ; es is not goot so long to sitz on de kalt grund; takes a bissel grog and youse goes on."

The new tavern, however, was built and ready long before the turnpike was a complete success, for many were the trials of the public spirited projectors of the enterprise. With the completion of the turnpike there came a demand for increased mail facilities. The government then engrossed with the French question and the impending war with that power, yet found time to accede to the demand

* Whoever trusts in God neither death nor Satan can harm.

SCENES ON THE LANCASTER TURNPIKE BETWEEN THE 43RD AND 45TH MILESTONES.

VIEW NEAR 45TH MILESTONE.   RUINS OF AN OLD LIME KILN.
AN OLD SIGN POST.

of the people. A post office was established in Downingtown April 1, 1798, the only one between Philadelphia and
Lancaster, and the official announcement was made that
there would be three mails per week between Philadelphia,
Downingtown and Lancaster, closing one-half hour before
sunset every Monday, Wednesday and Friday. This was
hailed with satisfaction by everyone.

In connection with the French war excitement of 1798
there is a curious anecdote. Early in the year envoys were
appointed to France by President Adams. One of these,
Callender by name, in place of embarking for France left
the city on a tour westward. Why or what for was not
known at the time. He got as far as Fahnestock's and
remained there several days, until on the morning of July
13th, when he was found by a teamster a little after day
break laying over 21st mile-stone dead—drunk.

The explanation of Commissioner Callender's strange
conduct is very simple when it is known that three fugitive
French Princes, Louis Phillipe, Duke de Montpensier and
the Count de Beaujolais, were at that time sheltered under
the humble, but hospitable roof of the old German Sabbath-
keeper. It would be difficult to imagine a greater contrast
than the home of these scions of French royalty at that
time with their former residence, viz., the Palais Royal at
Paris. The humble Roadside Inn, however, had this great
advantage, the three princes were as safe as the humblest
laborer in the land; their heads were safe on the shoulders
of their effete bodies.

It was to consult with these princes that Callender came
to the old Roadside Inn. The princes naturally did all
they could to favorably impress the Commissioner and
gain him for their cause. In this attempt they drew heavily
on their scant resources, plying the Commissioner liberally

with numerous bottles of old Madeira, which had been bought by Casper at Mather's sale and which it was claimed had come over the water, while yet the signboard bore the legend " Ye Adm'll Vernon."

It was in this eventful year (1798) that the capital city was again visited by the yellow fever scourge. A camp for patients was established beyond the Schuylkill, and donations of farm and garden produce were solicited. The Fahnestocks at once took active measures to collect and send the needed supplies to the sufferers, vieing with the Downings and Joseph Moore, of East Whiteland, in supplying the necessaries and luxuries to the sick and convalescent poor of the fever-stricken city.

After the road was finished and by its advantages and superiority over the common roads came into universal favor, with teamsters and travellers, the old tavern stands soon had more patronage than they could accommodate; this was especially the case with the Fahnestock's. Old Casper although having long passed the allotted period of three score and ten, still continued as host and proprietor of the house, holding to the German maxim that "No father should give the reins of his hands to his child as long as he lived." However, in 1789, old Casper then in his 77th year, was forced by the infirmities of age to relinquish the house to his son Charles, who was then in his 37th year, and in whose name the license was granted for the last year of the Eighteenth Century.

In the next year (1800), the present blacksmith shops were built on the turnpike. As before stated, the old shop on the Lancaster road stood in the meadow, about five feet north of the turnpike bridge. The top of the roof of the old shop was on a level with the low parapet of the present bridge and stood there for many years.

As has been mentioned in a previous article, during the period of 1790–1800 when Philadelphia was the capital of the United States, there were frequently delegations of the Indian tribes, who travelled up and down the road in their journey to visit the "Great Father"; on one of these visits an occurrence took place, which caused much speculation, and remains to the present day an unsolved problem, notwithstanding the many attempts made by the Fahnestock family and many others to solve the enigma. It was as follows: A short time after the turnpike was finished an Indian coming down the road had broken something about his gun, and, when he came to the Warren asked the smith at the shops to repair it. The blacksmith had just run out of charcoal, which was the only kind of coal then used by smiths, and told the Indian that he could not fix his gun until he had burnt a new kiln of charcoal. The Indian asked him if he would do it if he got him coal, and getting an answer in the affirmative he took up a pick and basket which were in the shops, and giving a grunt started for the woods on the South Valley hill. He returned in about half an hour with a basket full of black rocks or stones. The smith tried to make the Indian understand it was coal that he needed. The Indian merely put some of his black stones on the hearth and pulled the bellows, and to the surprise of the smith the stones commenced to burn. The Indian merely said, "White man now fix gun." The now thoroughly surprised smith found the Indian's rocks equal to his best charcoal. The gun was repaired, and the smith was naturally anxious to know where the burning stones were found, but nothing could induce the Indian to divulge where he had found it except that he said "there was much—much," pointing towards the wooded hillside. Many were the efforts made from that day to this to discover the location, but so far without success.

Although with the advent of the nineteenth century Philadelphia had ceased to be the capital city the traffic on the turnpike showed no diminution; our road became the great highway to the West. Stage lines were started to all points, while wagoning and emigrants increased to such an extent that ere long the licensed houses on the road between Philadelphia and Lancaster averaged one to the mile, and even then the farm houses adjacent to the highway were often called upon to accommodate the overflow.

When the political question cropped out in relation to the western territory, which culminated in the "Aaron Burr" fiasco, it became imperative as early as 1804 that regular communication should be maintained between Philadelphia and the Ohio at Pittsburg, other than by the always more or less uncertain post or express rider. Satisfactory arrangements, however, were not consummated until after much effort on the part of the federal authorities. The first notice of the new enterprise was the following quaint announcement—it was published in but a single paper, and is here reproduced in full as a contrast to the railroad advertisements of the present day—viz.:

PHILADELPHIA & PITTSBURG

MAIL STAGES.

A contract being made with the Postmaster General of the United States for the carrying of the mail to and from Philadelphia and Pittsburgh, in stage wagons, a line of stages will be in operation on the first of July next, on same route, which line will start from John Tomlinson's Spread Eagle, Market street, No. 285, Philadelphia, and from Thomas Ferree's, the Fountain Inn, Water street,

Pittsburgh; and perform the same route in seven days from the above places. Passengers must pay $20.00 each, with the privilege of twenty pounds of baggage, all above that weight, or baggage sent by above line, to pay at the rate of $12.00 per 100 pounds, if the packages are of such dimensions as to be admissible for conveyance.

The proprietors of this line of stages, well knowing the arduous undertaking of a new establishment, and aware of the laborious task and expense that the prosecutors of their necessary engagements will require, are determined that their conduct shall be such, as they trust will be sanctioned by a discerning public and receive their support.

Printed cards will be distributed, and may be had at the proprietors' different stage houses, giving a full detail of the distances and times of arrival at the several towns through which the line shall pass.

N. B.—Printers who shall think the above establishment a public benefit will please give the same a place in their respective papers a few times.

Philadelphia, June 13, 1804.

As announced in the above advertisement, promptly at 8 o'clock on the morning of the 4th of July, 1804, a fit day for the starting of the new national enterprise, the stage which was to be the first to run through from the Delaware to the Ohio was drawn up in front of Tomlinson's Spread Eagle stage office, then at the northeast corner of 8th and Market streets, the four prancing horses with bridles gaily decorated with red, white and blue ribbons. Long before the starting time the mail was in the "boot," the straps drawn tight, the booked passengers in their seats, while as a last precaution an extra keg of fistoil and tar was slung to the hind axle, the lynch pin examined and the dust proof

covers fastened over the hubs. Then after another glass
was drunk the driver and armed guard took their places
on the box, the lines tightened, the whip cracked and the
pioneer mail stage to the West left the stage office among
the cheers of the assembled multitude and whirled rapidly
out Market street towards Center Square, where another
ovation awaited the stage and its occupants from the citizens who were preparing to celebrate Independence Day.
The new permanent bridge was quickly passed and the
ironclad hoofs of the four prancing steeds clattered on the
smooth turnpike. At every tavernstand the passing mail
was received with cheers and wishes of Godspeed and safe
journey to the travelers. Stops were only made at such
stagehouses as the Buck, Eagle, Paoli, and there for liquid
refreshment only. It was near two o'clock in the afternoon, as the stage dashed down the Valley hill through the
toll gate at the twentieth milestone, when the guard blew
six sharp blasts on his bugle—this the signal to the host of
the "Warren" how many guests there would be for dinner; then came the notes of "Independence Day," the
"Yankee Doodle," the echo taking them up and returning
them through ravines on the hillside a hundred fold.
Hardly had the echo faded, when the four prancing steeds
were reined up in front of the "Warren." The stage door
was quickly opened, the passengers alighting and meeting
with a greeting as only Charles Fahnestock was capable of
extending to the wayfarer. The dust was quickly washed
down with cold punch, when dinner was served, toasts
drunk and ample justice done to the viands. In the meantime the anvil of the shops had been brought out into the
road and improvised as a cannon, and load after load was
fired in honor of the occasion. During the dinner the relays
had been brought out, and the stage was once more ready

for the journey westward. Another punch was drunk, hands shaken, and amid wishes of Godspeed, the reports of the improvised artillery, and the cheers of the assembled neighbors, mingled with the bugle notes of the guard, the stage with its freight started merrily up the hill on its way towards the Ohio.

This enterprise of running mail stages through to Pittsburg formed the theme of conversation for the balance of the week. Many were the different opinions pro and con —prophecies of failure and adverse criticisms; yet notwithstanding the headshaking and discouraging comments of Old Casper, the stage went through, arrived safely on time in a week, and the through mail was an established fact. These stages were what in later years was known as the " Good Intent Line." The route lay from Lancaster to Chambersburg, by way of Carlisle and Strasburg; arriving in Chambersburg in two and one half days, averaging about four miles an hour, from the latter place to the end of the journey; the progress under the most favorable circumstances was much slower, the distance from Chamersburg to Pittsburg, about 150 miles, taking four and one half days, or about two to two and a half miles an hour. There were thirty-five regular stopping places or stages between the two cities. At first the enterprise was slow in coming into favor with the traveling public. It was not until the following year (1805) that the proprietors were taxed to their capacity and were forced to run an occasional special or extra coach; this was necessitated by the excitement caused by the Burr Expedition, which had then reached its culmination; the success of the through stage line opened a new era for the Warren, and the house under the management of Charles Fahnestock, became known to travelers in this country and Europe, as one of the best kept houses in America. He was a rather spare built man, of 5 feet 11 inches, with a full beard, and always wore a brown or snuff-colored coat and spoke with a strong German accent. He was very particular in regard to the sale of liquors; ordinary local patronage and wagons were not encouraged. The bar was a small arrangement very high, and slabs running about 2 inches wide, and 3 inches apart, running from bar to ceiling. In front there was a small opening with an outside shelf holding about four glasses. The liquor was measured out by the gill or half gill and passed through this opening. When the landlord thought a patron had enough he would refuse him any more telling him quietly " to sit down awhile." The tavern keeper confined himself strictly within the old law of 1762 by which "Taverns were allowed to sell to regular inmates and travellers in moderation," (Acts Assembly, vol. 1, pp. 19–21—fol. Phila. 1762.)

The Fahnestock family had no sooner learned the principles and teachings of their guests than the Owens, Miss Wright and their followers were kindly and firmly informed by Charles Fahnestock that they would have to seek other quarters, that the house would afford them shelter no longer, nor would he harbor anyone who promulgated sentiments similar to theirs, which were so foreign to all religious and moral teachings. Another guest during the agitation of Owen's plan for colonization in the Great Valley was his Highness Bernhardt, Duke of Sachse-Weimar-Eisenach, who was then on a visit to this country. The attempt of Owen to interest the nobleman in his scheme resulted as did all of Owen's plans—in failure.

As before stated, local custom was not encouraged by the inn-keeper, regular habitues of the tavern were few, and such as there was were respectable and sober. Charles

Fahnestock was naturally a temperance man, and had the courage, when the house was at the height of popularity, to close his bar on Sunday. This was an unheard-of innovation at that day, which called down much adverse criticism upon him. He, however, persisted, and even went so far as to hang a sign over the bar

NO LIQUOR

SOLD ON THE

SABBATH

and he had enough moral courage to adhere to the determination. Among the few of the neighbors who were frequently to be seen on the tavern porch was an Englishman of means, Thomas Bradley, between whom and the innkeeper a strong bond of friendship had arisen. It lasted until death parted the two friends in 1829. Thomas Bradley was buried in the Fahnestock ground and is the only stranger who rests within the enclosure.

Another visitor who was occasionally to be seen at the Warren was Charles Fahnestock's cousin, Andrew. He was a Sabbatarian, and on account of his originality and appearance always attracted the attention of strangers. He always travelled on foot, dressed in a long drab coat, wearing a broad brimmed white hat, and carrying his long "Pilgerstab" (staff) in his hand. He was at one time quite wealthy, but gave all his wealth to the poor, saying "The Lord would never suffer him to want." He would never receive any salary for his services as preacher, trusting entirely in the Lord for his support. On these visits he would often take his cousin to task for joining the Presbyterian Church with his family and failing to keep the Sabbath (7th day), as had his ancestors before him.

The preacher on his journeys along the pike was often made the subject for the teamsters' jokes, who met him, but, as we would say at the present day, Andrew never got left. On one of these occasions, a teamster asked him if he believed in the devil. Andrew answered that "he read about him in his Bible." The wagoner then asked him if he ever saw the devil. The answer he got was, "I never want to see him plainer that I do just now." The ribald wagoner had no more questions to ask the German Sabbatarian.

At the commencement of the fourth decade (1830) travel had increased to such an extent that greater facilities and shorter time was demanded by the traveling public. To meet this demand the proprietors of the stage line, S. R. Slaymaker & Co., from Philadelphia to Chambersburg, and Reside Slaymaker & Co., from Chambersburg to Pittsburg, increased their stock and facilities to so great an extent that in 1831 they announced that they would henceforth run two daily lines to Pittsburg, viz.: The U. S. Mail stage, the "Good Intent Line," would leave their office, 284 Market street, Philadelphia, above 8th street, every morning at two o'clock a. m., for Pittsburg, via Lancaster, Harrisburg, Carlisle, Chambersburg, Bedford, Somerset and Mount Pleasant, going through in three days; only six passengers being admitted to each stage, as many stages were to be run as called for by the passengers, they averaging about six daily.

The Mail Telegraph stage line left Philadelphia at 6.30 a. m. by way of Greensburg from Bedford, making the trip in four days. This service was especially recommended to families or ladies, as the telegraph line avoided the fatigue of night travel. Firstrate horses, careful drivers and splendid new coaches were held out as the inducement to the traveling public. In September, 1831, during the height of the traveling season the tavern was discovered to be on fire. It was first discovered over the kitchen, and is supposed to have been caused by a defective flue or chimney. The whole structure soon fell a victim to the destroying element.

A curious anecdote in connection with the fire was long current. As soon as the alarm was given Charles called on several of the willing helpers to carry down the old German chest, which had belonged to his father, Casper. It was so heavy that it took five men to carry it. The innkeeper had it carried across the road. He then sat on it and calmly watched the destruction of his valuable property. His action at the time caused much comment. No information was vouchsafed. After the fire was subdued and the danger to the outbuilding over, Charles had the chest carefully carried to the house just east of the bridge, never leaving the chest out of his sight until it was again in a place of safety. The explanation to this was—the old German oaken chest was his bank, weighted down by the roleaux of gold and silver coin, which were stored between the folds of several old coverlids.

The house was at once rebuilt on the solid walls, which were unharmed by the fire, and on its completion enjoyed an increased patronage.

In the month of April, 1834, the Philadelphia and Columbia Railway was open for travel. For a time the Green Tree had been the eastern terminus for the stages. So far the Warren had not felt the effects of the new improvement. Within a month after the first train went down the road drawn by the "Black Hawk" matters changed. The stage coaches were withdrawn east of Columbia. It was the twentieth of May, a dark rainy day, when the last regular stage passed the Warren on its way eastward. The Fahnestocks, similar to many other tavern keepers who were off the railway, had no faith in its ultimate success. The various local stages still ran, so did the Pitt teams, but neither were accustomed to stop at the Warren, nor could the old tavernkeeper bring himself down to cater to that class of custom. For a while a stage was run from the West Chester intersection to the Warren for the benefit of such travelers who wanted to stop at the Warren, but the arrangement was soon discontinued. Charles Fahnestock, now well-advanced in years and disgusted with the existing state of affairs, turned the inn over to his son William, who had become a strict Presbyterian and member of the Great Valley Church, much against the wishes and advice of his "Uncle Andrew," who was wont to tell him that all of his plans would "go aglee" unless he returned to the faith of his forefathers and kept the seventh day. William, however, turned a deaf ear to his relative, and became a prominent man in the church. Beside being active in all church matters, he was for some years the "precentor" and led the singing.

Wm. Fahnestock had presided over the inn not quite three years when his father was gathered to his people, and was buried with his father in the old family plot on the Valley hill, the Rev. Wm. Latta consigning the body to the grave. It is said that this was the last interment in the ground.

William now had full sway, and as he was a strong temperance man he at once stopped the sale of liquor, and to the surprise of the frequenters of the pike a new sign board appeared in front of the "Warren," not high up in the yoke as of yore, but flat in front of the porch. It was an oval sign hung on pivots and fastened with a hook. During six days of the week it read:

WARREN

TEMPERANCE

HOTEL.

At sundown on Saturday the sign was turned and until Monday it read:

NOTHING

SOLD ON THE

SABBATH.

The new departure did not meet with favor, and the patronage of the house rapidly decreased. The new host, in his temperance idea, eventually went so far as to cut down the large apple orchard which was in the field opposite the house, south of the pike. This was done so as to prevent the apples being used for cider. The year after the experiment of keeping a temperance hotel failed— summer boarders were tried with varying success. William also made several attempts to locate the traditionary coal mine of the Indian, shafts were sunk at different points on the South Valley hill, but were eventually abandoned. He also went extensively into the *Morus Multicaulis* craze* which ended in failure. It seemed, as if not only the glory of the house had departed, but that the prophecy of the old Seventh-day Baptist preacher, "Uncle Andrew," was coming true.† So in the next year, 1838, Wm. Fahnestock divided the tract up and sold it to various parties, the tavern and adjacent fields being bought by a Mr. Thompson, who kept it one year and then sold it to Professor Stille, of Philadelphia, who in turn sold it in 1846 to the present owners.

* The silkworm craze.
† *Vide* p. 77, supra.

6

❡N part XXIII of the
NARRATIVE AND CRIT-
ICAL HISTORY OF THE GER-
MAN INFLUENCE IN THE
SETTLEMENT AND DEVELOP-
MENT OF PENNSYLVANIA,
published in Volume XXI of
the Proceedings of the Pennsylvania-German Society, an
extended history was given
of two of the famous inns on
the Lancaster Turnpike, both
of which were kept by Pennsylvania-Germans.

These two papers on the Spread Eagle and Warren
Taverns, as before stated, were a part of a series prepared
by the present writer for the *Village Record* of West
Chester during the eighties of last century, much of these
facts and traditions being gathered by the writer in his boy-
hood days, prior to the Civil War.

Owing to the widespread interest aroused by the republication of these sketches, and in compliance with the requests received from many sources, the Pennsylvania-German Society concluded to reprint the remaining papers
of this series, thus giving the history of the old "Blue

THE WAYSIDE INNS ON THE LANCASTER ROAD.

NORTH QUEEN STREET, IN LANCASTER,

As seen on entering from the north. The Court House is seen in the distance.

1836

Ball" in Tredyffrin—originally the "Half-way" house between the Schuylkill and the Brandywine. Then the eleven taverns on the turnpike between the Spread Eagle Tavern, near the milestone and the Paoli Tavern, just above the Landmark. Thence follows the Story of the Paoli, the "Green Tree," a short mile west of the Paoli, and of the "Ship" in West Whiteland, near the milestone. To these is added a sketch of the Old "White Horse" Tavern in East Whiteland. The views illustrating these papers were taken by the writer prior to 1886.

One of the results of the publication of the story of these old inns in our former volume is a renewed interest in these old landmarks, by the residents along the main line of the Pennsylvania, and a proposition that suitable tablets, appropriately inscribed, be put up along that ancient highway, marking places of historic interest, prominent among which are the sites of a number of these ancient hostelries, as well as other buildings connected with the early history of this section of Pennsylvania.

THE BLUE BALL TAVERN, ON THE OLD LANCASTER ROAD, IN TREDYFFRIN TOWNSHIP, CHESTER COUNTY.

N Tredyffrin township, on the borders of Easttown, about a mile west of the village of Berwyn, just south of the railroad, where the turnpike crosses underneath the iron highway, formerly stood in a slight ravine or valley formed by a spur of the valley hill, a primitive stone house, roughly built of the stone found on the surface of the ground during the first quarter of the eighteenth century. It was located on the south side of the provincial road, which was then the only means of reaching the outlying settlements towards Conestoga. Remains of this ancient building may yet be seen in the rear portion of Robert Glenn's house, the front, or main portion of the old Inn only having been demolished when it was replaced by the present house in 1863. In the earliest part of our

THE WAYSIDE INNS ON THE LANCASTER ROAD.

"YE PLOUGH," 13 M. 3 QRS.
"YE WHITE HORSE," 26 M. 1 QR.
AN OLD TAVERN SHED.
"YE BLUE BELL," 19 M. 3 QRS.
WITH DISTANCE FROM SECOND AND MARKET STREETS, PHILADELPHIA.

PHOTOS. BY JULIUS F. SACHSE, 1896.

history this house was a prominent landmark and known as the "Half-way House," it being about equidistant from the Schuylkill (Coultas) ferry and Downing's Mill (now Downingtown) ; it also occupied the same position on the road connecting the two Welsh congregations of the Church of England, viz.: St. David's (Radnor) and St. Peter's (Gt. Valley).

From 1735 when the house came into the possession of Robert Richardson it became known as the "Blue Ball," under which name the original house as well as its successor, a few rods north on the turnpike, attained more or less celebrity a century later. In the primitive days of our province a roadside tavern was a necessity, not only as a house of entertainment but one of shelter as well. These roadside inns were among the prominent and important landmarks on the early maps of the province, as may be seen by reference to Scull and Heaps's map published in 1750, or any of the early distance tables in use a century and a half ago, on which our inn is stated to be 19 miles, 3 quarters, and 62 perches west of the Court House in Philadelphia. The road on which the Blue Ball was located was the most important public road in the province of Pennsylvania. In Colonial days it was the main road from Philadelphia to Lancaster and was known as the "great" or "provincial" road; to the present generation it is known as the old Lancaster Road in such places where its bed is not occupied by the turnpike or where it has not been vacated altogether.

Tradition tells us that a portion of the road which is in Chester county was formerly an old Indian trail, and became one of the first roads in the primitive settlement.

The road does not seem to have been opened through to Lancaster until after 1730, as in January of that year the

Magistrates, Grand Jury and other Inhabitants of the
County of Lancaster, presented a petition to the Provincial Council, setting forth "that not having the Con-
veniency of any Navigable water, for bringing the Produce of their Labours to Philadelphia, they are obliged
at a great Expense to transport them by Land Carriage,
which Burthen becomes heavier thro' the Want of Suitable
Roads for Carriages to pass. That there are no public
Roads leading to Philadelphia yet laid out thro' their
County, and those in Chester County, thro' which they
now pass, are in many places incommodious. And therefore praying that Proper Persons may be appointed to
view and lay out a Road for the Publick Service from the
Town of Lancaster till it falls in with the high Road in
the County of Chester, leading to the Ferry of Schuylkill
of High Street, and that a Review may be had of the Said
Publick Road in the County of Chester." The prayer of
this petition being granted Thos. Green, George Ashton,
William Paschal, Richard Buffington, William March,
Samuel Miller and Robert Parke of the county of Chester,
or any five of them, together with the same number from
Lancaster county, were empowered jointly to review the
said high Road and report to the board what alterations
may be necessary to be made therein, to suit the Conve-
niency of Carriages and for the better accommodation of
the Inhabitants of the Province.

The Commissioners made a report to the Council at
Philadelphia Oct. 4, 1733, setting forth that they had laid
out the road to the house of John Spruce, in Whiteland
township, Chester county, a distance of thirty-two statute
miles from the Courthouse in Lancaster. They concluded
their report:

"And we further beg leave to say, that being unprovided with a copy of the Records of the aforesaid public road through Chester county, and the lands contiguous to the said road being mostly improved and at present under corn, we find ourselves incapable to discover where the same hath been altered from its true course (to the Damage thereof) and also conclude the present season of the year improper for a review."

January 23, 1735–6, a petition was presented to the Council by sundry inhabitants of the townships of Tredyffrin, Easttown, Willistown and places adjacent to the County of Chester, setting forth that the road is brought no further than to the house of John Spruce in Whiteland township, in the County of Chester, to the great inconvenience of persons travelling with wagons and other heavy carriages and therefore praying that orders may be given for perfecting the said road, in pursuance to the order granted on the above petition.

It was, however, not until November 23, 1741, that the survey of the road was completed. In this report it mentions that the road was run by way of William Evans's smith shop then in Tredyffrin Town to the sign of the Ball, thence it entered East Town, &c. The road was confirmed and ordered to be opened and cleared forthwith.

The winter of this year (1741) was an exceptionally hard one, and was noted for the frequent and deep snows, interrupting all travel and communication between the settlers for weeks at a time. The severity of the winter was complained of everywhere throughout the province, in many places in Chester county cattle died from want of fodder; many deer were also found dead in the woods, while some came tamely to the plantations and fed on the hay with the other cattle. Toward Lancaster county the snow averaged over three feet in depth, consequently the settlers suffered much for want of bread, all access to the mills being barred by the deep drifts, in many cases families of new settlers had little else to subsist on but the carcasses of deer they found dead and dying in the swamps or runs near their houses.

In the early times before the "Great" road was opened, all travel was on horseback, all freight and merchandise was transported on pack horses, grain was carried to the mill or market in large sacks holding between two and three bushels, which were placed on pack saddles, and a boy mounted on one horse would lead three or four in a line behind the one he rode. By means of these pack horses the most unwieldy articles such as bars of iron, barrels of liquor, and other necessities were also transported. Women generally rode behind their male companions on a pillion attached to the hinder part of the saddle, and secured firmly on the horse. High horseblocks were a necessity and could be seen in front of most all houses. It was not long before road carts were built and by the middle of the century wagons came into use for transportation but on account of their clumsy and cumberous construction did not entirely supersede the pack horse until many years later.

Peter Kalm, the Swedish naturalist, who visited and traveled through the province in 1748, in writing about the customs and condition of the country says: "The roads are good or bad according to the difference of the ground. In a sandy soil the roads are dry and good, but in a clayey one they are bad. The people here are likewise very careless in mending them. If a rivulet be not too great, they do not make a bridge over it, and travelers may do as well as they can to get over. When a tree falls across the road it is seldom cut off to keep the road clear, but the people go round it."

Richardson kept the Inn until 1741, when the property was bought by Thomas McKean, an uncle of Governor McKean; he without difficulty obtained a license and appears to have kept the house until 1752. In the following year he was succeeded by Conrad Young, of Philadelphia. It seems that the new landlord was a German, and on his accession to the property changed the name to the "King of Prussia." He continued in possession until 1757. The traveling public and residents do not seem to have approved of the change on the sign-board, so the Inn continued to be known as the "Ball." During the August term of 1758 we find the petition of Joseph Wilkinson, late of Uwchlan at the Red Lion, in which he represents "That your petitioner is removed to the place where the sign of the Blue Ball has long been kept (now the King of Prussia), on Lancaster road, where he proposes (under your favor), to continue to keep a Public House of Entertainment."

During 1759 Joseph Wilkinson was again licensed. It was during the term of Young and Wilkinson that the French and Indian excitement was rife in the Province. There is a tradition that a part of the forces under General Braddock, as well as the more fortunate Generals Forbes and Stanwix, were assembled and mustered at this place prior to their joining the main body on its march to the Ohio; in corroboration of this tradition it was customary to refer to the very high doors with arched heads in the old tavern stables (demolished and replaced by present barn in 1863), which were said to have been built so high that the King's troopers could ride in and out without dismounting. During 1758-9, when requisitions were issued in the county for horses and wagons for military purposes the appraiser for Easttown, Tredyffrin and the adjoining townships, it is said, had his headquarters at the "Ball," further that on account of the opposition of the Quaker element his office was anything but a sinecure.

March 13, 1759, Dr. Bernhard Van Leer, of Marple, purchased the Blue Ball property from Conrad Young, who had again returned to Philadelphia. The two plantations connected with the tavern contained 209 acres. The following year, 1760, Dr. Van Leer leased the property to Benj. Weatherby, who in August of that year petitions for a license when "a public house of entertainment has been found necessary in Tredyffrin for over twenty years past on the road leading from Philadelphia to Lancaster." Among his recommenders we find Francis Wayne, Isaac Wayne, Thomas McKean, &c. Weatherby continued from year to year until 1766, the names of some of the leading vestrymen of both churches before mentioned being among his recommenders. It frequently depended upon who appeared as the recommenders of an applicant, whether the license was granted or refused. As early as 1763 an application was made to the Governor for the regulation of taverns, in which it sets forth "That one only should be in such a defined distance, or in proportion to so many inhabitants, that the bar rooms should be closed upon the Sabbath day, as it would tend to prevent youth from committing excesses to their own ruin and injury of their masters and the affliction of their parents and friends." In 1767 Weatherby was succeeded by his widow, who asks renewal and continues until 1771, in August of which year Philip Upright presents a petition setting forth that he "has rented the Tavern late in the tenure of the Widow Weatherby where an old and well accustomed house of public entertainment has been kept for a number of years known by the name of the "Blue Ball." Among the signers were Isaac Wayne, Anthony Wayne, John Gronow, Griffith Jones and others.

By the following interesting account of a "trip for pleasure" over the old road during the summer of 1773, taken from the diary (lately found) of a person whose name is unfortunately lost to us, the initial XI .... only being given,[1] one may well contrast the present luxurious mode of travel between the two cities, with the long, weary and uncomfortable journey which awaited the seeker for pleasure a hundred and thirty-nine years ago.

"Left Lancaster about three o'clock in the afternoon on Wednesday, the 25th, a fine, pleasant day, in good spirits, but alas, a sad accident had like to have turned our mirth to mourning, for W. driving careless and being happily engaged with the lady he had the pleasure of riding with, and not mindful enough of his charge, drove full against a large stump which stood in the way, by which the chair was overturned, and the lady thrown out to a considerable distance, but happily received no hurt. This evening about 8 o'clock arrived at Douglass', (between Millers and The Hat,) where supped and rested all night. The supper was pretty tolerable, beds indifferent; being short of sheets for the beds the woman was good enough to let W. have a tablecloth in lieu of one.

"Thursday 26th, 1773, at 7 o'clock left Douglass; about ten arrived at the Ship (west of Downingtown) where we breakfasted, which was good, the people obliging, the house clean and decent; at 11 o'clock set out; at one we stopped at the Adm. Warren thence proceeded to Stradleburgs(?) during which time it rained vere heavy upon us, which was the more disagreeable, as the ladies were much exposed thereto, neither of the chairs having tops; soon after our arrival about four left Stradleburgs, and were all the way down in a heavy rain; but happily the ladies' good constitutions,

1 Penna. Mag., July, 1886.

prevented bad effects following their being so much wet; about eight o'clock we arrived at the city."

Philip Upright continued as landlord of the Blue Ball probably until the invasion by the British, September, 1777, when he was despoiled of his possessions along with the other unfortunate residents of Tredyffrin who chanced to come within reach of the hireling foe. There are no official records during the three following years as to who was the host at the inn.

In July, 1777, the first attempt was made to run a "Stage Wagon" between Philadelphia and Lancaster, but as it took two days to travel the distance of sixty miles, the experiment was soon abandoned. The condition of the great road at this time was so bad as to be almost impassable, wagons could not carry more than half or two thirds of a load on that account. The causes of this state of affairs were two-fold; first, the great amount of travel caused by the demand for supplies for the subsistence of the armies; second, the impossibility of getting the inhabitants to make the necessary repairs. In some of the worst places details of the militia were sent to make the needed repairs, under the direction of the Deputy-Quarter-Master-General of the Army, still this gave but partial relief. Numerous complaints were made to the Supreme Executive Council of the State early in the year, while Washington and the army were yet quartered at Valley Forge. In May, 1778, the Council took action upon the complaints and at once issued the following order to all Supervisors in both Lancaster and Chester counties:

"Lancaster. May 7th, 1778.

"Whereas, complaints are made to Council that the Roads and Highways in this State are ruinous, and in many parts almost impassable, for want of being repaired and amended, as the Law requires, whereby Travellers are impeded in their Journies, private Business obstructed, and the publick supplies for the Army delayed, and their Operations in Danger of being disappointed, to the great Scandal, Detriment and Danger of this Commonwealth and the manifest injury of the common cause of America:

These are therefore to require and command all Supervisors of the Roads and Highways within this State, without Fail or Loss of Time, to proceed to the Reparation and Amendment of the Roads, and to enjoin upon all Magistrates and others concerned, to exert themselves in making presentments of Defects and Nuisances in the premises or to the Quarter Sessions of the peace of the respective counties, or to prosecute and otherwise proceed against all deficient Township and Supervisors according to Law, that they may be punished in such manner as their neglect shall require."

By Order of Council.

By this increased travel on the provincial road the roadside Inns reaped a considerable harvest both before and after the British occupation of Philadelphia and this vicinity. As an illustration of some of the curious customs of those times, the following tavern rate is given, as published in the *Philadelphia Evening Post,* Sept. 11, 1778. These prices no doubt were in Pennsylvania currency and were fixed by the County Courts as a matter of protection to the traveller.

"Prices as fixed by the Court of Quarter Sessions for Philadelphia county, September 7th, 1778, to be paid in Public Houses within said county:"

Madeira wine per quart..............£2	0	0
Lisbon wine per quart............... 1	5	0
Tenriffe wine per quart............. 1	5	0

Spirit per gill........................	3	9
Brandy per gill.......................	3	9
Whiskey per gill......................	1	3
Good Beer per quart..................	1	6
Cider Royal per quart................	2	6
Cyder	1	3
Punch per bowl of about three pints....	12	6
Toddy per bowl of about three pints....	7	6
Breakfast of Tea or Coffee...........	3	9
Dinner	5	0
Supper	3	9
Lodging	1	3
Good hay for horse per night..........	3	9
Oats per quart......................		7

Any householder exceeding the above to be fined 20s for first offence; 40s for second offence and for third offence £5 and loss of license. The rates of the County of Philadelphia generally regulated the adjoining counties.

Attempts at highway robbery at this period of the Revolutionary struggle were of frequent occurrence; reports of any notice of highwaymen being in the vicinity would have the effect of preventing travelers from starting alone on their journey or after dark. This was especially the case during the time in which the noted Captain Fitz and his satellite Dougherty were wont to place travelers on the provincial road under tribute, as frequently happened between the Blue Ball and Caln. The boldness of this marauder caused the Executive Council July 13, 1778, to offer a reward of one thousand dollars for his apprehension. This resulted in the capture of Fitz, August 22, at Castle Rock, about six miles from the Inn.

By reference to some memoranda found in the "Remembrances of Christopher Marshall" it is to be inferred that during the four years following Upright the Blue Ball was kept by Captain Thomas Reese, who in 1777 lived on an adjoining plantation in Tredyffrin, his claim for losses sustained by the British being still in existence. Reese is mentioned by Marshall in January and September, 1778, and again in July, 1780.

Under date of Sept. 12, 1778, we find: "Reached Capt. Reese's tavern at the Blue Ball by dusk. Here we took up our residence for the night. We drank coffee for supper and slept in our great coats, stockings, &c., for fear of 'fleas and bugs.'"

Sept. 13. "We rose early, fed our horses, I paid the reckoning, thirty-eight shillings and ten pence; set off for Lancaster, &c."

The winter of 1778-9 was an exceedingly mild and pleasant one. It was so mild that in our vicinity on the 22d day of March, the orchards of different kinds were all in blossom, and the meadows as green as in the month of June; however on the next morning a storm came from the northeast and before noon there was nearly two feet of snow on the ground; this "cold snap" destroyed all the fruit for that year.

In 1782 John Phillips was the tavernkeeper and continued until 1787. After the successful close of the Revolutionary struggle, travel continued to increase to so great an extent, as to make transportation extremely expensive and difficult on the road.

In 1790 over 150,000 bushels of wheat passed over the road from Middletown for the Philadelphia market. This was exclusive of the large amount of grain raised in Chester and Lancaster counties which was also brought down the same avenue. At this time the cost of transporting a bushel of wheat from the Susquehanna to the

Schuylkill was £2 6d; it was further calculated that from one third to one half of the weight of the wheat was carried back in salt, liquors and other merchandise at 5s per hundred weight. In connection with this matter of increased transportation, the grain consumed as horse feed became an object of great attention. It was calculated that these 150,000 bushels of grain at forty-five bushels to a wagon load, were equal to almost three thousand and fifty loads; and as each team was not less than ten days on the road, it consumed ten bushels of rye, which is equal to over thirty-five thousand bushels of that grain.

As has been above mentioned the difficulties and expense of this transportation increased with the increase of the travel. The wear and tear on the teams and wagons was enormous. The terrible condition of the road especially during a wet season can now hardly be described; the ruts in the miry road often hub deep, it was nothing for teams to be stalled in the mud for half a day. During winter and spring it was even worse and it was not an unusual occurrence for wagons to freeze fast in the ruts, and there remain until they could be gotten out when the frost came out of the ground in the spring. Teamsters beside their freight were required to carry several days' forage for their horses (this was usually rye), also a drag chain about ten to twelve feet long, axe, shovel, clouts, a gallon keg of tar and oil, usually swinging under the back axle, extra horseshoes, nails, hames, strings and lynch pins, and a mattress for themselves completed the equipment. In addition some of the more frugal carried their own provisions.

In 1784 and again in 1788 efforts were made to establish a line of stage coaches between Philadelphia and Lancaster, but the enterprise proved futile on account of the wretched condition of the highway, the great amount of travel, combined with the uncertainty of arriving at the end of the journey in any reasonable time.

The activity along the road caused a number of houses to be erected along the roadside between the Blue Ball and the Spread Eagle, two miles below. Of these houses not a trace or vestige remains to denote their former location or existence, with possibly a single exception of an old house standing just below Berwyn station, where the road connecting the turnpike and State road crosses the old road. This house prior to the building of the turnpike in 1792-5 was used as a public house and known as the " Fox " Tavern It later did duty as a country store.

Dr. Van Leer the owner of the Blue Ball property died early in 1786 and by will devised the Blue Ball Tavern, in Tredyffrin, with two tracts of land, 100 acres and 80 acres, to his daughter Mary, wife of Moses Moore who kept the Tavern from 1788 to 1792. Governor Mifflin's message of the latter year contains the following curious allusion to tavern licenses and their collection.

" I again bring to your notice the impediments in the collection of the duty on tavern licenses; and to point out the expediency of placing on a better footing the mode of compelling the officers, who are intrusted with public monies, to account as it may at present happen, that the process can only be issued by those who are them-selves, the delinquents."

A gentleman stopping at this Inn during the winter of 1793 and writing about the winter pastimes in the country says: " The chief amusement of the country girls now is sleighing, of which they are passionately fond, as the snow is not expected to lay on the ground very long. The consequence is, that every moment that will admit of sleighing is seized with avidity. The tavern and inn keepers are up all night, and the whole country is in motion. When the snow begins to fall, our planter's daughters provide hot sand, which at nights they place in bags at the bottom of the sleigh. Their sweethearts attend with a couple of horses and away they glide with astonishing velocity; visiting their friends for many miles around the country. But in order to have a sleighing frolic in style, it is necessary to provide a fiddler, who is placed at the head of the sleigh, and plays all the way. At every Inn they meet with on the road, the company alight and have a dance."

The three following years, 1793–6, John Llewellyn was the tenant. In the meantime the new turnpike had been built, and at once became the great highway of travel. At this point the turnpike was located about five hundred feet north of the former road and a considerable stretch of the old road was vacated. This cut off the old hostelry almost completely from its patrons. The erection of more modern and comfortable public houses, situated directly on the new turnpike also made serious inroads on the business of the old Blue Ball. Notwithstanding these drawbacks John Werkizer obtained license for the years 1797–8–9.

It was not long before this deflection of the travel and patronage induced the owner of the property to erect a new tavern under the same name directly on the turnpike.

OLD INNS ON THE LANCASTER ROAD SIDE.

THE ELEVEN HOTELS WHICH FORMERLY STOOD ON THE LANCASTER TURNPIKE BETWEEN THE EAGLE TAVERN AND THE PAOLI INN.

"**H**ERE is to the Sorrel Horse that kicked Unicorn that made the Eagle fly; that scared the Lamb from under the Stage, for drinking the Spring-house dry; that drove the Blue Ball into the Black Bear, and chased General Jackson all the way to Paoli." This unique toast, a favorite one with the hardy teamsters, who teamed along the turnpike prior to the railroad era, enumerates all the taverns in the east end of Chester county, in the order in which they came. The first three were in Radnor township, Delaware county, the others in Easttown and Tredyffrin townships, Chester county. The "toast" will no doubt be recalled to the memory of many an old "stager" who followed the road in those by-gone days;

perhaps some may also recall the eccentric character who was credited with organizing it, viz.: "Old Joe Pike."

The necessity of the Public House for the entertainment of Man and Beast, as well as the important position which it occupied in the community in these early days, may be judged from the fact that the eleven inns enumerated in the above "toast" were all within a distance of five miles. The first tavern beyond the Spread Eagle was the "Lamb"; this house was in Easttown township, about 300 yards east of the fifteenth milestone. It was built at the commencement of the last century by the owner of the property, George Reese, who was afterwards High Sheriff of Philadelphia. The west or main end of this house was the original "Valley Baptist" Church, the precursor of the present remodeled edifice. When the old log church was sold it was bought by Reese, taken down and re-erected as stated above, and stood there until about 1878 or '79 when the house was altered to its present condition. Shortly after the completion of the turnpike the building was used for several years as a country store by one Jonathan Jones, until 1812 or '13 when John Lewis of the "Stage" received a license to keep a public house at that location. He continued there for two years, when he was followed by Jacob Clinger, who erected the stone part of the house and kept the inn for many years, being succeeded to the business by his son Henry until after the advent of the railroad, when the house ceased to be profitable. This house always enjoyed a good reputation as a wagon stand and took considerable of the surplus travel, which could not be accommodated at the Eagle. The sign-board of the house swung from a high pole representing a rural landscape with a fine lamb in the foreground.

The next house, "The Stage," just west of the fifteenth

milestone, was located on the crest of the South Valley hill, and it was claimed to be the highest point west of Philadelphia. It it not known by whom this house was built, but it was owned by Dr. Harvard Davis, while John Lewis of the Lamb kept the house as an inn in 1810. He remained for two years, when he was succeeded by Edward Robinson, he in turn by Col. Alex. E. Finley, during whose term a number of militia musters were held on the Glassley Commons, between the Stage and the Lamb. As prominent actors in these gatherings Ensign Hampton, Captains Weatherby and Rowan will no doubt be remembered by some of the older residents. While Finley was the landlord of the Stage, Sammy Stirk was the wheelwright at the shops at the fifteenth milestone; he was also Constable. Among the hangers on about the tavern there was a poetic genius, name now forgotten, who had received an official visit from Stirk, when under the impulse of the moment he dashed off the following at the Constable's expense:

> As Pluto was taking an airing one day,
>   My noble Carlisle fell plump in his way;
> On the plains of famed Glassley these friends they
>   did meet,
>   And they very politely each other did greet,
>
> Good morning, said Pluto, with a sarcastic smile,
>   I am happy to meet you, my noble Carlisle;
> For you and your master must instantly go,
>   Through the mouth of old Ætna to the regions
>   of woe.

The name of the last landlord was "Shoeneman" usually a synonym for the Stage in the latter years—during which time it dropped lower and lower in the scale; rough and tumble fights and brawls being of nightly occurrence. The sign-board that swung from a tall pole and depicting a stage-coach drawn by four prancing horses, as well as the sign of the Lamb, were the work of a local artist, a self-taught genius, one James McGuigan, who lived on the Glassley Commons; when he died Col. Isaac Wayne wrote his obituary heading it with a verse of "Grey's Elegy."

The next hostelry was the "Spring-house" Tavern. This inn was the successor of the "Fox" Tavern on the old road mentioned in a previous article. John Llewellyn the owner of the property was also the landlord of the Blue Ball from 1793 to 1796, and it is known that his brother David kept the "Fox" until 1804, when the property was sold to William Torbet. It is thought Torbert or his son Alexander was the builder of the house on the turnpike, but it does not seem to have come into prominence until after 1814, when the house and property came into the possession of the Kugler family in which it remained until 1861, when it was conveyed to John McLeod. Remains of this old hostelry may still be seen in what is now known as "McCloud's" house in Berwyn, between the turnpike and railroad, a little east of the lumber yard below the Station. The old Spring-house for a time enjoyed considerable patronage while under the direction of the Kuglers. For a time, about 1825–30, the name was changed to the "Gen. Washington," this was after the house had been leased to John Dane; however, the residents of the vicinity as well as the patrons and habitues refused to recognize the change on the sign-board, so the house continued to be known as the "Spring-house," but in later years after the decline of the turnpike, the house was usually called "Peggy Dane's" after the widow and successor of the last lessee; the house at one time was partly destroyed by fire.

After leaving the "Spring-house" the wagoners toiling up the pike would next pass the "Drove" usually kept by some member of the "Reese" family. This inn was almost opposite the sixteenth milestone, and as its name implies was mainly intended as a "drove stand." The proprietor catered principally to that class of patrons. One of the traditions connected with this cabaret was that the "Drove" on the turnpike and the former inn by the same name, which stood on the old road (in Cuckolds-town) a little north of the subject of this sketch, were connected by an underground passage. This house, next to the "Ball," probably enjoyed the least enviable reputation in the township. The various accounts of the large amounts of money lost at hazard, the frequent brawls and fights, which finally culminated in the killing of Nathan Reed by one J. V., soon affected the custom of the tavern. This house after the building of the railroad, which at this point necessitated a cut of over twenty feet deep, was turned into an institution of learning, which under the supervision of Professor Noble Heath, attained considerable celebrity. It was known as the "Reeseville Boarding School." It flourished with variable success until 1850, when the school was discontinued. The old inn was finally torn down in 1869 and replaced by the present handsome residence built by the late owner, H. Fritz.

The next inn was the "Ball," the successor of the celebrated colonial tavern of the same name, which was located for so many years on the old provincial road and the bridle path which preceded it through the wilderness. The "Ball" on the turnpike was built probably in the first years of the last century, and will now be easily recognized as "Old Prissey's" so called after the last owner, who was also the daughter of the builder of the house. This house is about three fourths of a mile west of Berwyn, and when built had but two stories, the upper story with the semi-circular windows being a later addition after the house had been partially destroyed by fire. There are many gruesome and ghostly tales told in connection with this house, probably more than about all other inns on the turnpike put together. The late owner who died over twenty-five years ago, after a stormy existence of almost or more than a century, is usually the chief actor in these legends. The house itself in a dilapidated condition as it now appears (1886) still has an uncanny look about it. The half-round arched windows have been likened to wicked half-shut eyes.[1] Still no matter how eccentric Old Prissey was the fear with which her appearance would inspire school children, or how she scolded when angry, the writer still would fain draw the veil of charity over the old soul and not believe many of the deeds attributed to Old Prissey.

One characteristic tale about Mrs. Priscilla however is too good to be passed. When the railroad was built it was located very near her house. While horses were the motive power all was well and good; this lasted from 1834 to 1836—but when in the latter year the problem to employ steam as the motive power on the road was successfully solved, the trouble commenced. Prissey saw her business dwindle and decrease while her competitors at the Paoli but a short distance beyond prospered. She soon got very crabbed about this loss of patronage; of this fact the railroaders soon became aware. As sure as a train would come along, so sure was Prissey out scolding the

---

[1] The house of late has been modernized and is now used as a suburban residence.

crew. They in turn would return her compliments with shrill whistles. The war of shrieks came to a climax when her pet heifer one day strayed on the railroad in front of an approaching engine. The result of this act was disastrous for the bovine. The rage and anger of Prissey knew no bounds. As her claim for damages was not at once settled to her satisfaction, she got her revenge as follows: the tallow was all rendered out, and after dark a good proportion of the killed cow was put on the rails. No train passed the house that night, but it is said an engine with its train kept at it until the water gave out. (Locomotives of that early day were of little power and carried no sand.) The next day this brought down the State Collector from Paoli, and another

OLD " PRISSEY "
As the writer knew her.

war of words ensued, but Prissey with her arms akimbo defied them all and told them they either had to pay her or take the cow as she chose to give it to them—on the rail whenever she pleased. Before the sun set that day Prissey had her "shinplasters" (State bank notes) safe in her possession.

Priscilla Moore is said to have been married several times—Edw. Robinson, John Cahill, John Fisher, but she was usually known as Mrs. Robinson, and the old Inn as "Mrs. Robinson's."

The next wagon tavern was the Black Bear with its swinging sign-board. It stood at the crossing of the road from Howellville, on the corner opposite Schofield's store. Little is remembered of this house except that it was a tavern on the old provincial road before the turnpike was built, and that in later years it became a great stand for sales and vendues. It continued a licensed house until 1857, Hugh Steen being the last landlord. George Steibler, Jos. Morgan and Elisha Worrall were at different times in charge. The house was torn down about a half century ago; the sign on the inn was the usual swinging sign with the name painted in large gilt block letters on a black ground. The old pump still standing by the wayside is all that remains to mark the spot of a former busy gathering place on the turnpike. Before leaving the "Bear" the writer would call special attention to the fact that at several points between the Blue Ball and the Warren, three miles above, the steel rails lie exactly in the old and forgotten Indian trails, those narrow paths unmarked by blaze on tree or pile of stones, which over two centuries ago led through the unbroken forest, in the sombre shades of which the aborigine would disappear on his hunting or depredatory excursions. This trail after the advent of the Caucasian, successively became the cart road—great road 1741—turnpike 1792—State road 1832, and finally part of the Pennsylvania Railroad system in 1852.

[*Note.*—Since the above chapter has been put in type, the following interesting, additional matter relating to the Old Black Bear, just below the eighteenth milestone, was received from Prof. George Morris Philips, Principal of the State Normal School at West Chester, whose great-grandfather, John Philips, kept the old Black Bear tavern just below Paoli, and died there in 1790. He is down in the Pennsylvania Archives as a first lieutenant in the Revolutionary Army. An old descendant of his, Hibberd Chalfant, of Atglen, Chester County, recently stated that he remembers very distinctly when a boy six years old his grandmother telling him again and again that John Philips served as a Captain through the Revolutionary War, that he was in a prison ship, almost died from illness, and that his wife was allowed to go to the ship and nurse him, and doubtless saved his life. As he heard, she was also very helpful to the other sick soldiers there. Upon his recovery he was sent home to recruit, probably exchanged and, greatly against her wishes, insisted upon reentering the army, and served through the war. Chalfant's recollection is that this ship on which he was confined was on Lake Champlain. Our earlier information however, always was that he was in the prison ship *Jersey,* in New York harbor and that according to British records he died there, but the records in the Brooklyn Historical Society show that he survived, as he certainly did. He died intestate and his widow administered his estate, and her account is filed in the Chester County Court House and is very interesting. Professor Philips has possession of a fine old eight-day clock which formerly belonged to Capt. John Philips and was made by J. Garrett, of Goshen. It was bought at a sale of his effects by Prof. Philip's grandfather for his own son, John M. Philips, and now really belongs to his grandson, William P. Philips, of New York City.]

With the " Bear " end the wagonstands in Easttown and

Tredyffrin east of Paoli; the next house west was the "General Jackson Inn," a first-class stage tavern, built by Randall Evans, who also owned the Black Bear; he was a brother of Gen. Joshua Evans of the Paoli; after Randall's failure he was succeeded by Evanson, who rechristened the house "The Franklin," under which name it has been known to the present generation; it was also in later years known as the "Evanson House," and used for summer boarders until the repurchase in 188– by John D. Evans the owner of the Paoli.

This house was noted from 1821–29 as the meeting place of Farmers' Lodge, No. 183, A. Y. M.

A curious tale is told in connection with one of these old wagon stands which was up for sale. A wanderer coming down the turnpike, barefooted and sunburned, having all the appearances of a roustabout, his shoes and coat hanging from the staff carried across his shoulder, when in front of the inn stopped, and after reading the sale bill went into the barroom and asked the landlord, in a broad Pennsylvania dialect, "to let him *emol the haus see.*[1] The Innkeeper judging from the appearance of the man, that he merely wanted to see the house for the purpose of planning a possible nocturnal visit in the future, told him curtly to clear out and go about his business. The tramp, after some grumbling to himself, went on his way down the pike. A week or more elapsed. In the mean time the property had been sold at the Exchange, in Philadelphia, when our country Dutchman again arrived in front of the inn, but this time coming from the opposite direction. Again stopping in front of the house, and after carefully scanning the outside of the house and outbuildings he went into the bar, and on being asked by the host what he

---

[1] See the house.

wanted, answered, after some deliberation. *Er docht er wol des hause nan emol angucke.*² On being asked jeeringly, whether there was anything else that he wanted, he replied in broken English that the landlord had better get out himself as he was now the owner of the house, at the same time producing to the consternation of the now surprised landlord, the title papers for the property. It is needless to say that the manner of the tenant at once changed towards the new owner.

But three of the houses mentioned in the wagoner's toast, viz.: The Eagle, Jackson and Paoli, ranked as stage taverns of reputation with the travelling public, the others were what were known as Wagon Taverns or Drove stands. These taverns were an entirely different institution, from the well kept stage taverns previously described; each one had its particular class of patrons, and the landlord made it a specialty to cater to their particular needs and requirements; no benefit would accrue at the present day to repeat any of the gruesome tales of crime and tragedies said to have been committed within the precincts of some of the less respectable of these roadside inns; yet among some of the older residents of Easttown there are still dim memories of tales current in their younger days, of the disappearance of a peddler or two at one of these houses or at another where it was said that the chances of any drover who stopped at the inn, arriving at the end of his journey with a full purse were very slim; the writer, however, after diligent search of the Court records has not been able to find a single case of that kind coming to the official knowledge of the Court. Still there is no doubt that at some of these cabarets it would have been very unwise for a lone traveller, known to have a large sum of

---

² He thought that he would look the house over.

money in his possession, to stop and remain over night, especially if he were addicted to the social glass and not particular about his company.

The wagoner's Inn as its name implies was patronized mainly by that hardy class of men, who made a business of transporting flour, grain and the products of the West to Philadelphia, while on the return trip they would carry merchandise and other freight for the merchants of the inland country. Many of these wagoners were farmers and tilled the soil during the Spring, Summer and early Fall, when after the crops were all in, they took their teams and went on the road as wagoners until the next Spring's work commenced. It is a matter of record that many of our farmers or their sons by this means cleared the incumbrances off of their homesteads.

When the teamster came to the tavern where he intended stopping for the night his first care was to go into the barroom and see whether there was still a desirable corner vacant on the floor for his mattress or bed; if so the mattress was put on the floor and woe to any one who attempted to displace it. After refreshing himself with a "jigger" of rum invariably measured out to him by the attendant back of the bar, which was in direct contrast to the traveller who stopped at the stage tavern who was always privileged to either pour out his own liquor or specify the quantity he wanted in his grog, the teamster would then give his attention to his team. The wagon would, if possible, be run into the yard and the horses placed on each side of the tongue, on which a trough with their feed was placed. This was done to save the expense of stabling. After the team was thus provided for, the men would get their supper, after which they would congregate in the barroom or on the porches and the evening passed in drinking and card playing. Fights and brawls among them were of frequent occurrence; this was especially the case in the lower class of these wagon taverns, where the turmoil would often run riot during an election or other times of public excitement.

A traveler who passed a night at one of these inns during the election period in 1818 says the tavern was filled by drunken men, who made a frightful uproar and yielded to excesses so horrible as to be scarcely conceivable. The rooms, the stairs, the yard, all were filled with drunken men and those who were still able to get their teeth separated uttered only the accents of fury and rage.

Scenes similar to the above were no doubt of frequent occurrence and were not to be wondered at when it is taken into consideration that there were frequently over thirty teams gathered around a single inn, the conductors of which as a class were inured to exposure and excesses; together with the usual employees and habitues of the particular inn and the large quantity of strong liquor it was then the custom to drink.

Besides the wagoner, these inns afforded shelter and accommodation for the drover with his herds of stock on their way eastward. Emigrants on their way to the far West, as it was then called, the present generation know it as Ohio, would also stop at these inns for economy sake. It was then the custom for a family seeking a new home west of the Alleghenies, to start out in a wagon; this contained, besides the family, their few household goods and such farm implements as could be conveniently carried. These teams rarely consisted of more than two horses. In warm, fair weather the emigrants would sleep in their wagon, by the roadside; the stop was usually made near a spring or creek, where a fire would be built and the scanty meal prepared by the wife, while the husband foraged around with his grass knife procuring fodder for his horses. Roustabouts, "tramps" we now call them, would also frequent the bar and inn yard whenever the opportunity presented itself. These with the hired men from the neighboring farms made up the patronage of this class of public houses.

The landlords of these taverns were a peculiar race, brought forth by the times, and many of them exercised great power in political and county affairs, noteworthy examples of whom were General Joshua Evans, of the Paoli, and Col. A. E. Finley, of the Stage.

The earliest information in reference to the establishment of and customs at these inns, known to the writer, are several letters written early in March, 1795, shortly after the completion of the turnpike. This writer says: "I sat out from Philadelphia on horseback, and arrived at Lancaster at the end of the second day's journey. The road between Philadelphia and Lancaster has lately undergone a thorough repair, and tolls are levied upon it to keep it in order, under the direction of a company. This is the first attempt to have a turnpike road in Pennsylvania, and it is by no means relished by the people at large particularly by the wagoners, who go in great numbers by this route to Philadelphia from the back parts of the State. On the whole road from Philadelphia to Lancaster, there are not any two dwellings standing together, excepting at a small place called Downing's Town, which lies about midway. The taverns along this turnpike road are kept by farmers, and they are all very indifferent. If the traveller can procure a few eggs with a little bacon, he ought to rest satisfied; it is twenty to one that a bit of fresh meat is to be had, or any salted meat except pork. Vegetables seem also to be very scarce, and when you do get any, they generally consist of turnips, or turnip tops boiled by way of greens.

"The bread is heavy and sour, though they have as fine flour as any in the world; this is owing to their method of making of it; they raise it with what they call 'sots'; hops and water boiled together.

"The traveller on his arrival is shown into a room which is common to every person in the house, and which is generally the one set apart for breakfast, dinner and supper. All the strangers that happen to be in the house sit down to these meals promiscuously, and the family of the house also forms a part of the company. It is seldom that a single bed room can be procured, but it is not always that even this is to be had, and those who travel through the country must often submit to be crammed into rooms where there is scarcely sufficient space to walk between the beds. No dependence is to be placed upon getting a man at these taverns to rub down your horse, or even to give him his food, frequently therefore you will have to do every thing of the kind for yourself if you do not travel with a servant, and indeed even where men are kept for the purpose of attending to travelers, which at some of the taverns is the case, they are so sullen and disobliging that you feel inclined to do everything with your own hands rather than be indebted to them for their assistance; they always appear doubtful whether they should do anything for you or not, nor will money make them alter their conduct.

"It is scarcely possible to go one mile on this road without meeting numbers of wagons passing and repassing between the back parts of the State and Philadelphia. These wagons are commonly drawn by four or five horses,

8

four of which are yoked in pairs. The wagons are heavy, the horses small and the driver unmerciful; the consequence of which is, that in every team, nearly, there is a horse either lame or blind. The Pennsylvanians are notorious for the bad care which they take of their horses. Except the night be tempestuous, the wagoners never put their horses under shelter, and then it is only under a shed. Each tavern is usually provided for this purpose. Food for the horses is always carried in the wagon and the moment they stop they are unyoked and fed whilst they are warm. By this treatment half the poor animals are foundered. Most people travel on horseback with pistols or swords and a large blanket folded up under their saddle which they use for sleeping in." Michaux who went over the road a few years later in 1802 draws a similar picture. There was apparently but little if any improvement during the seven years which had elapsed. He states: "The taverns along the road are almost everywhere very bad, nevertheless, rum, brandy and whiskey are always to be had, these articles of provision being considered as being of the first necessity, and the profits of those who keep taverns arise principally from the liquors of which there is a very great consumption. At breakfast they serve up bad tea, worse coffee and small slices of fried ham, to which are sometimes added eggs and boiled fowl. Dinner —a piece of salt beef and roast fowls, with rum and water for drink; at night coffee, tea and ham. There are always several beds in the rooms in which they sleep, while sheets are seldom met with; happy the traveller who arrives on the day they are changed."

As to table manners it was the usual custom for guests to reach across the table, or across three or four persons sitting next to them when they wished for some particular dish. It was also the custom at these inns to do the carving with one's own knife and fork, or spoon when wanting sugar; in other words the patrons of the dining room helped and looked out for themselves, and it was understood to be each man's duty to see that he got at least his share of the meal, even if he did choke to death on the first mouthful of meat, as was the case once at the old "Stage."

During the latter part of the first quarter of the century there was on the entire length of the turnpike an almost unbroken procession of the ponderous Conestoga wagons, each drawn by five or six strong horses, on which was transported all the merchandise destined for the interior, and the extensive travel thus created and concentrated upon this once splendid highway stands without parallel in the history of transportation in the country previous to the introduction of steam power. In contrast with the present methodical system of transportation the following advertisement, in 1818, of an old forwarder may prove of interest to the present generation. It reads:

THOMAS M. SOUDER

HAVING OPENED A STORE

No. 312 Market Street

For the reception of Merchandise to be transported to the

WESTERN COUNTRY IN WAGONS,

offers his services to the Merchants generally to take charge of their goods to be forwarded to Pittsburgh or any part of the western Country. He flatters himself that by his attention and the experience he has acquired he will be enabled to give general satisfaction.

There were two occurrences which were always sure to break the monotony of the daily routine at these inns and which would empty the barroom of its inmates in an exceedingly short time. One of these events was the competition between the rival stage coach lines. These races were of common occurrence on the turnpike in fine weather, and the favorite coach would always be sure of a cheer from the motley throng assembled on the tavern porch, as the foaming steeds dashed by the inn. The other event was the arrival or departure of the accommodation stage. This, as its name implies, stopped at all points wherever a passenger beckoned to the driver. These stages stopped at most all wagon taverns along the road. They were patronized as it were principally by parties who were going but a short distance, or those who could not afford to travel by either "post" or "mail." This sort of stage was generally a two-horse vehicle, the driver was also on terms of intimacy with both host and frequenters of these inns. Another source of revenue of the driver was the carrying of parcels or packages between any points on his route. These parcels would be delivered for a small remuneration and the custom was in fact the precursor of the present "Express" system.

Travel in these stages was anything but comfortable, no matter how pleasant it was in one of the large four-horse mail stages; this was particularly the case in wet weather. A traveler giving his experience says: first, his feet got wet, and his clothing became plastered with mud from the wheel, the curtains not being tight; then the men's coats and boots commenced to steam in the confined coach, the horses draggled and chaffed by the traces, while the driver got soaked both inside and outside, while his temper was tried and found wanting. Still the tribulations of the traveler in the stage wagon were insignificant in comparison with what awaited the traveler in an "accommodation" sleigh, which was substituted for the stage when the ground was covered with snow to a depth which precluded the stage from making headway. This sleigh was often a machine gotten up for the nonce, and consisted merely of rough boards nailed together in the form of an oblong box, with a drapery and roof of common muslin. There were narrow cross boards for seats, on which the passengers were compelled to sit bolt upright, without any support of any kind. This was not comfortable, but when the snow was smooth and firm, the machine rattled on very fast and smoothly over the icy road.

One of the greatest drawbacks to the travel in winter on the turnpike were heavy snow storms; these often interrupted stage as well as wagon travel for days at a time, the mails as well as travelers being often detained at roadside inns for days on account of the deep drifts. The two greatest snow storms on record since the building of the turnpike were probably January 23, 1804, and the one in January, 1831; the latter is known as the great snow storm. It commenced on the night of the 14th of January and continued without intermission until about noon on the 16th, during which time it is supposed the snow fell to an average depth of three feet. The wind was very high during the storm and the snow drifted in many places into banks over twenty feet high. Occupants of stage coaches and wagons who were on the road and were overtaken by the storm were forced to abandon their vehicles, leave them in the road and seek shelter for themselves and animals from the elements at the nearest inn or farm house, and in many cases when, after the storm had ceased and the parties went out to remove the stages or wagons, no sign of them could be found, the drifts having completely covered them up. On the turnpike the snow in many places had so drifted to fill up hollows and form banks in many places from five to ten feet high, rendering the road impassable. This of course stopped all transportation for almost two weeks; and notwithstanding the herculean efforts made by the mail contractors to open communication it was a week before the first mail arrived at Lancaster from Philadelphia. After the snow had ceased the contractors at once attempted to force the road from the Schuylkill to the Spread Eagle with several companies of horsemen of from twenty to thirty in each party, but so deep were the drifts that, with the violence of the wind and lightness of the snow, every mark of their progress was immediately obliterated, and the road as impassable as before. At the Lancaster end the situation was even worse. All travel was abandoned for the time being, although every exertion was made to forward the mail. Fifty horses were employed in the vain attempt to break the road in advance of the stage over a distance of nine miles, yet the stage could not proceed, though dragged upon runners by six of the finest horses of the line, one of which perished through exhaustion. An idea of this storm may be formed by the fact that the cut for the railroad in front of the Drove Tavern in Reeseville (Berwyn) which had just been completed (it averaged 22 feet in depth) was so completely filled up with snow as not to be discernible.

This storm was particularly severe on a number of German emigrants who were on the road to Ohio with their families and possessions. They were cared for by the county authorities until the roads were in condition to permit their journey Westward. A gentleman who was anxious to get to Lancaster at this time thus describes his experience: "I remained a fortnight waiting for a change of weather but it never came, the roads, however, had become quite practicable for traveling and I at length determined on departure. At five o'clock in the morning I accordingly drove to Market street, where I took possession of a place in a sleigh shaped like an omnibus. The snow lay deep on the ground and the weather was cold in the extreme. After some delay the vehicle got into motion. The mail sleigh in which I found myself a passenger was one of the most wretched vehicles imaginable. The wind —a northwester—penetrated the curtains of the machine at a thousand crevices, and charged with particles of snow so fine as to be almost impalpable communicated to the faces of the passengers the sensation of suffering under a hurricane of needles. We breakfasted at a wretched cabaret, and the pretensions of the dinner house were not much greater. The fare, however, though coarse, was abundant, still a traveler, to get on comfortably, must take things as he finds them." In connection with this phenomenal storm, the following description of some of the tribulations which beset the hardy class of men in the inclement season, who handled the reins of the mail coach, will no doubt prove a revelation to many a youth of the present generation: "When the existing circumstance rendered it impossible to proceed further with the stage he (the driver) unloosed the horses and endeavored to take them to the nearest inn, a distance of about a mile and a half. He rode about half a mile when his four horses became imbedded in a snowbank. They were so perfectly chilled that they were almost incapable even of walking, much less of extricating themselves. Under these circumstances, he procured a rail from an adjoining fence, and dug them out of the snow. He then retraced his steps, depositing three of his horses in a neighboring stable, and with the other continued his journey determined as he said 'to deliver the mail safely at the hazard of his life.' When he arrived at the inn, his eyelashes were cemented together with ice—himself so benumbed that he could scarcely articulate, and his situation so precarious that the most active restoratives were found necessary for his recovery."

The era of transportation by wagon which developed into such large proportions, and in which so much individual capital was invested and required, and gave employment to so large a number of horses and men, may be said to have reached its height about 1830, and from the 18th day of October, 1832, when the first car was drawn over the Columbia Railroad, from Belmont to the West Chester Intersection, we may say that the transition from the Indian "Trail" to the "T—rail" of modern civilization was complete. As far as our vicinity was concerned the decline of the wagon calling was rapid, and as a natural result the patronage of what little travel remained on the turnpike after the railroad fairly got under way was soon absorbed by the more reputable hostelries.

Chairman Miller in his report on Internal Improvements made to the Legislature in 1834, thus sets forth the situation of affairs in this transition period:

The disposition of men to frequent long established marts, and to travel to them on the beaten path, is not suddenly overcome. Old habits are not readily abandoned; old associations not easily broken up; a sudden transition from one course to another can only be induced from powerfully interesting motives. The trader is frequently interested in the employment of the wagoner. The railroad system is not fully adapted to the demands of a trade, the extent of which can only be determined by its own development. Delays occur, discontent ensues, the parts of the system are not in harmony with each other; the system is formed and completed, and moves harmoniously and hand in hand with the demands made upon it. The smaller asperities are smoothed down, gradually— the old disappears and the new takes its place, and as the keel boat has been displaced by the steamboat on the waters of the West, so will (but not to the same extent), the wagons disappear and be displaced by the railroad car on the line of the railroad.

The hardy wagoners got up a song upon the loss of their occupation, a verse of which ran:

" Oh, 'tis once I made money by driving my team,
    But now all is hauled on the railroad by steam.
    May the devil catch the man that invented the plan,
    For its ruined us poor wagoners and every other man."

By the " every other man " were meant the inn keepers, blacksmiths, hostlers and such others who depended on the travel on the turnpike for a livelihood.

The following wail published about seventy years ago will form an appropriate close to this sketch:

" Not only have the Conestoga teams disappeared but the stage. Alas! the stage horn no longer is heard—the bounding wheels no longer rattle over the white compact road.

" No more the weary stager dreads
    The toil of the coming morn;
    No more the bustling landlord runs
    At the sound of the echoing horn,
    The old turnpike is now left alone,
    And the stagers have sought the plow.
    We have circled the earth with an iron rail,
    And the Steam King rules us now."

" THE GENERAL PAOLI."

AND THE EARLY DAYS OF THE TURNPIKE AND THE COLUMBIA RAILROAD.

IN the early part of the eighteenth century while yet Anne reigned over England there arrived in the Delaware river a staunch ship, name of craft and master long forgotten, with a number of Welsh emigrants, who had been allured from their native shores by the fair and seductive promises of Wm. Penn and his agents. These people came to the new world in the hope of bettering their condition, supposing they were to have here a barony of their own; they possibly also expected like many of their fellows who had preceded them to these trackless wilds, to find kinsfolk in the Indians, who they were told by their local sagas and legends were descended from their countrymen, who were supposed to have settled two colonies in the western world as far back as the twelfth century, under the leadership of Prince Madog, the youngest son of

PHOTO. BY JULIUS F. SACHSE, 1885.

THE "PAOLI."
VIEW FROM THE WEST.

Owain Gwynedd, a King of Wales. This tradition was further strengthened by the supposed or fancied similarity between the language of the Leni Lenape and the ancient "British" tongue, which was the only language in use among the rural Welsh. Among these emigrants, who thus landed on our shores was a little family group, from "Merionethshire"; they were first cousins, and all of one family, forty-two in number. Our records unfortunately fail to inform us how many of this remarkable family were either left behind in Wales or died during the long voyage across the stormy Atlantic.

This family group soon after their arrival scattered themselves through the Welsh tract in Chester county, mainly in the great valley, others again settled on portions of what is known as Montgomery county, at that time, however, part of Philadelphia county. Their settlements can still be traced by the Welsh names given to their new homes at the purchase of the land.

These settlers brought little to this country in the way of worldly possessions; in many instances their entire fortune besides a few household goods, and the means to purchase a plantation, consisted solely in their rugged constitutions and their "Pedigree," which by the aid of the prefix "ap" they traced back to the original Adam of old.

One of the most prominent of this family group was one William Evans, who we find in 1719 purchased a plantation of five hundred acres in the upper portion of the "Welsh Tract" located on the south valley hill in the southwestern part of the township of Tre: yr: Dyffryn, signifying in their musical language "Stony Valley." William Evans was a blacksmith by trade and here started the first smithy in the vicinity. His shop and house, which was probably a rude log structure, was located near the

old bridle path to Conestoga which was the precursor of
the old Lancaster road. From the earliest time he was a
man of considerable importance in the infant settlement,
and he appears as a vestryman together with his neighbor,
Anthony Wain (Wayne) the immigrant, in the first regular vestry formed in 1725 at the old Welsh Church in
the lower end of the Welsh Tract (St. David's, Radnor).
His son, Joshua Evans, born 1732, was probably the
builder of the oldest part of the present stone tavern,
which at that time, though a small and unpretending
structure, was destined to become famous and known far
and near, and to have a name in history as long as the
country shall last. It was the sign-board of this house
which gave the name to the barbarous affair during the
Revolution, on the night of September 21, 1777, although
the massacre took place much nearer to the Admiral
Warren than to the subject of our sketch. The name of
"Paoli" is always associated with the unfortunate affair.
This was really the result of the accidental naming and
locating the house on the military map drawn just after
lished in London during the following year.

The house at the time of the Revolution was a small
unpretentious two-story affair, with small windows and
low ceilings and, as near as can now be determined after
the lapse of one hundred and thirty-five years, covered a
space of about 42 x 30 feet. Remnants of the original
building can still be seen. The house when built faced
the ancient road leading from the Yellow Springs to Newtown Square and known as the Darby road. It is also said
to have been a former Indian trail. This road crossed the
old Lancaster road at an angle at this point. The house
stood some distance north of the old Lancaster road, now

supplanted by the turnpike. The course of the former road can still be traced through the hollow where the pumping station stands, thence westward up the hill by a row of cedars just back of the Church of the Good Samaritan. The house did not appear as a landmark until long after the Revolution.

In the August session of the Court of General Quarter Sessions held at Chester in 1769, the following petition was presented to the Judges:

"The petition of Joshua Evans Humbly Showeth. That whereas there is no house of public entertainment between the Yellow Springs and the Square in Newtown, on the road leading through a large body of the upper part of this country by the Valley Church[1] to Chester, Darby, &c., which is too great a distance for one stage, being fourteen miles apart, and of consequence must be attended with great disadvantage to the large concourse of people passing that way and as your petitioner has a very commodious house situated in the township of Tredyffrin, on Lancaster road, where the aforesaid road meets with the same, as the great road leading down through Newtown to Darby and Chester branches therefrom, and as your petitioner humbly considers a public house in the aforesaid place would be of great use not only to those passing to Chester and Darby, but also to travelers going and coming that way from Philadelphia, &c., &c., your petitioner therefore humbly requests your Honors to recommend him to his Honor, the Governor, for a license to keep a public house of entertainment in the aforesaid place and your petitioner as duty bound shall ever pray.

(Signed) JOSHUA EVANS.

The recommenders signing this document were Anthony Wayne, Lewis Gronow and sixteen others, most all of them being prominent members of the Valley Church.[1]

The petition, however, it is said was strenuously opposed by the widow Weatherby of the Blue Ball, one mile east of the new candidate for public patronage, as well as by Lynford Lardner, the landlord of the Admiral Warren, two and a half miles further west, who in his petition to the Court in 1770 sets forth that he was but three and a half miles from the Blue Ball, and that there was no necessity for the new tavern which had been set up in the previous year between his place and the Ball.

Notwithstanding this strong opposition to the recommendation of Evans for license, the Judges seem to have thought that an inn was necessary at this point, and the application was endorsed "allowed"; they were probably influenced in their action by the good character of the applicant, together with the known respectability of his recommenders.

No doubt the patriotic spirit then rife in the province had something to do with the selection of the name of the inn. The new tavern was called "The General Paoli Tavern."

It was named after Pascal Paoli, a Corsican General and patriot, who at that time was living in exile in England, and who though unsuccessful was still the ideal patriot and champion of liberty of the day.

In 1755 Paoli had been elected generalissimo of the Corsicans, who were then struggling against the Genoese; he waged the war so successfully as to confine the enemy within the narrow limits of their fortified seaports. His next care was to enact wise laws, introduce reforms, and encourage agriculture. But all his noble labors were rendered abortive by the Genoese selling the Island to France. After a heroic struggle against the invaders Paoli once more became an exile. Very little is known of the Paoli tavern during the first years of its existence; it was not until the outbreak of the Revolution that the new tavern came into prominence, owing to the proximity of the house to the homes of Anthony Wayne, Rev. David Jones, the Bartholemews, Andersons, Gronows, Pearces, and other patriotic minded men of the vicinity. The inn soon became a favorite gathering place of the patriots; meetings were held, when the affairs of the province and the situation were talked over and plans laid for future action.

No records remain us as to the losses sustained by the owner of the Paoli while the country was overrun by the British after the battle of the Brandywine, in September, 1777. The history of the affair on the night of the 20th of September, one and a half miles southwest of the inn, known in history as the "Massacre of Paoli," is too well known to repeat here. On that eventful night were two regiments of British troops (the fortieth and fifty-fourth infantry) under the command of Colonel Musgrave, stationed at the road crossing here, so as to intercept the patriots should they attempt to retreat in this direction; these troops were not in action during that night.

After Philadelphia was evacuated by the British forces in June, 1778, the Paoli, together with all the roadside inns on the way to Lancaster, commenced to reap the harvest caused by the great increase of travel on the great road from Philadelphia.

It was no doubt about this time that the first addition was made to the house. This addition is still discernible in the rear of the large house; it was built of limestone or blue marble of the Valley, the joints were pointed; it was about 27 x 30 feet and the house still fronted on the Valley road, the gable end being towards the Provincial road.

This enlargement became necessary on account of the

increased demand upon the landlord, the house at that early day already having attained a reputation for clean beds and good cheer for man and beast.

The following curious extract relating to the Paoli is from the diary of William Priest, who was a musician and a member of the Philadelphia theater in 1794–6 and it well illustrates the local gossip of the times:

"August 10, 1794, we slept about a mile from the 'Pioli,' I took a walk to reconnoitre the field of battle, with one who was present at that horrid affair."

"General Wayne was completely surprised, but had his revenge at Stony Point.[1] I spent the evening at the 'Pioli,' with a surgeon of the American army lately from the scene of action; he gave me a disgusting account of the misunderstanding that subsists between the American citizen on the frontier, and their neighbors in Upper Canada. It seems the Canadians are accused of assisting the Indians in their decisive action against 'St. Clare.'"

It was not until after the completion of the turnpike in 1794 that the era of great prosperity of Paoli commenced.

Local tradition gives to General Anthony Wayne the credit while a member of the General Assembly of the State, 1784–6, of offering the first resolution relating to the improvement of the roads and inland navigation of the State.

The turnpike was located so as to run directly in front of the tavern, and as the old road was vacated for a considerable distance in both directions it naturally brought all the traffic upon the new highway directly to the house.

This great road, the first of its kind in America, was 62¼ miles long, twenty-four feet of the bed was covered with a stratum of pounded stone eighteen inches thick in

---

[1] St. Peter's P. E. Church (Great Valley).

THE WAYSIDE INNS ON THE LANCASTER ROAD.

THE BIRTHPLACE AND HOME OF GEN. ANTHONY WAYNE.

ONE-HALF MILE SOUTH OF THE "PAOLI".

the middle of the road, and decreasing each way to twelve inches. The valley hill was the most elevated and steep on the road but the angle of ascent nowhere exceeded four degrees; the highest point on the road is the top of the hill just west of the Paoli, and is said to be six hundred feet above tide water.

The act incorporating the Philadelphia and Lancaster Turnpike Company was approved by Gov. Mifflin April 9, 1792, and states that

"Whereas the great quantity of heavy articles of the growth and produce of the country and of foreign goods which are daily transported between the city of Philadelphia and the western counties of the State requires an amendment of the highway, which can only be effected by artificial beds of stone and gravel disposed in such a manner as to prevent the wheels of carriages from cutting into the soil, the expenses whereof will be great, and it is reasonable that those who will enjoy the benefits of such highway should pay a compensation therefor, and there is reason to believe that such highway will be undertaken by an association of citizens if proper encouragement be given by the Legislature."

"Elliston Perot, Henry Drinker, jr., Owen Jones, jr., Israel Whelen and Cadwallader Evans, of Philadelphia, and Edward Hand, John Hubley, Paul Zantzinger, Mathias Slough and Abraham Witmer, of the County of Lancaster, were appointed Commissioners to open books and receive subscriptions to the stock, the par value of each share being $300, after notice had been given in two English and one German paper in Philadelphia and the paper printed at Lancaster, for one calendar month of the time and places when and where the books were to be open to receive subscriptions. On these days the Commissioners were obliged to attend and permit and suffer all persons who shall offer to subscribe in the said books, which were to be kept open at least six hours in every Judicial day, for three days if necessary; on the first of these days, any person, of the age of twenty-one years shall be

9

at liberty to subscribe for one share; on the second day, for one or two shares; on the third, for one, two or three shares; if not all taken by the end of the third day the Commissioners were empowered to adjourn until all shares are subscribed when the books are to be closed. Each subscriber was required to pay a deposit of thirty dollars per share."

The annual meetings of the new company were held on the second Monday in each year at such places as decided on by the stockholders. Section VIII. authorized the surveyors, etc., of the company to enter into and upon all and every, the lands, tenements and enclosures, through and over which the said intended turnpike may be thought proper to pass, etc. The course to be pursued in making the road was to combine shortness of distance with the most practicable ground from the west side of the Schuylkill, opposite Philadelphia, so as to pass near to or over the bridge on Brandywine creek, near Downing'stown, from thence to Witmer's bridge, on Conestoga creek, thence to the east end of King street, where the buildings cease in the borough of Lancaster.

From among the curious provisions and regulations, as set forth in the Act incorporating the company the following are selected:

By Section IX. the employers or agents of the company were authorized to enter upon the lands in, over, continuous, and near to which the route and track of the intended road shall pass to dig, take and carry away any stone, gravel, sand or earth there being most conveniently situated for making or repairing the said road.

The next section gives authority for the construction of permanent bridges wherever necessary; it further states that the company "shall cause a road to be laid out fifty

feet wide, twenty-one feet whereof in breadth at least shall
be bedded with wood, stone, gravel or any other hard sub-
stance, well compacted together a sufficient depth to secure
a solid foundation to the same; and the said road shall be
faced with gravel or stone pounded in such manner as to
secure a firm even surface, rising towards the middle by
a graded arch, and so nearly level in its progress as that it
shall in no place rise or fall more than will form an angle
of four degress with a horizontal line.

Tolls were authorized to be established and collected at
the completion of every ten miles of road, after a favorable report of same had been made to the Governor by
three skillful and judicious examiners.

The company were empowered to appoint their toll
gatherers who had the right to stop any person from passing over the turnpike until they had paid their toll. Tolls
were all based on a stretch of ten miles, and so in proportion for a greater or lesser distance, viz.:

For	every	score of	Sheep,	⅛	dollar.
"	"	"	Hogs,	⅛	"
"	"	"	Cattle,	¼	"
"	"	Horse and rider, or led Horse,		1-16	"
"	"	Sulkey, Chair, or Chaise with one horse and two wheels,		⅛	"
"	"	Chariot, Coach, Stage, Wagon, Phaeton, or Chaise, with 2 horses and four wheels,		¼	"
"	Either	of the Carriages last men- tioned, with four horses,		⅜	"

For every other Carriage of pleasure, under whatever name it
may go, the like sums, according to the number of wheels and
horses drawing the same.

For every Cart or Wagon whose wheels do not exceed the

breadth of four inches, ⅛ dollar for each horse drawing the same.

For every Cart or Wagon whose wheels shall exceed in breadth four inches, and not exceed seven inches, 1-16 dollar for every horse drawing the same.

For every cart or wagon, the breadth of whose wheels shall be more than seven and not more than ten inches, or being of the breadth of seven inches shall roll more than 10 inches, five cents for every horse drawing the same.

Where the breadth shall be more than 10 inches and not exceed 12 inches, or being 10 shall roll more than 15 inches three cents for every horse.

For every cart or wagon where the breadth of wheel shall be more than 12 inches two cents for every horse drawing the same.

Between December 1 and May 1, no wagon with four wheels, having less than four inches breadth of tire was to be leaded over 2½ tons,

From four to seven inch tire 3½ tons,
   "   seven to ten   "   5   "

For carts with two wheels the limit was
under four inches 1¼ tons
From   "   to seven inches 1½ tons,
   "   seven to ten   "   3   "

From the first of May to December 1 the limit was about one half ton more to the wagon or cart.

It was further ordered, that no cart, wagon or carriage of burden whatsoever whose wheels shall not be the breadth of nine inches at least, shall be drawn or pass over the said road or any part thereof, with more than six horses, nor shall more than eight horses be attached to any carriage whatsoever, used on the said road; and if any wagon or other carriage shall be drawn along the said road by a greater number of horses, or with a greater weight, than is hereby permitted, "one of the horses attached thereto shall be forfeited to the use of said Com-

pany to be seized and taken by any of their officers or servants, who shall be at liberty to choose which of the said
horses they may think proper, excepting the shaft or wheel
horse or horses."

In charging tolls two oxen were estimated as one horse,
" and every mule as equal to one horse."

Section XVIII. authorized the managers to increase
above tolls if at the expiration of two years the profits did
not amount to six per cent. At the end of ten years a
report was to be rendered to the Assembly, of their
accounts for the three preceding years, and if it should
appear that the clear profits and income would bear a
dividend of more than 15 per cent. per annum the tolls
were to be reduced, so as to reduce the dividend down to
15 per cent. per annum.

The company was further enjoined to erect posts and
sign-boards at all intersections, also to place milestones on
the roadside beginning at a distance of one mile from the
east side of the Schuylkill; also at every toll gate, a placard
placed in a conspicuous position showing in legible characters, the distance from Philadelphia, the distance from the
nearest gates in each direction, designating the number of
miles and the fractions; also, a printed list of the rates
of toll, which, from time to time, may lawfully be
amended.

Drivers were ordered to keep the right hand side in the
passing direction. The fine for obstructing the road, or
passing on the left side was two dollars and costs.

In a subsequent Act approved April 17, 1795, the company were empowered to increase the width of the road to
sixty-eight feet. The Act also made it unlawful for the
company to demand or receive any toll for a greater distance than shall be actually traveled; it further provided,

that no toll was to be paid by persons for passing on the road upon the business of their adjoining farms.

Before the construction of this road regularity of transportation was impossible, as during the rainy season, or on the breaking up of the frost, wagons were frequently detained on the road sometimes for weeks, and the merchandise conveyed in them was subject to injury from the delay as well as the roughness and dangerous condition of these highways. It was further calculated that the reduction in the expense of transportation, added to the increased value of the lands adjacent to the great turnpike, would amount to more than the cost of its construction.

On the new road broad wheeled wagons, such as were known by the name of "Conestogas," "Turnpike Schooners" or "Pitt teams" were supposed to carry thirty barrels of flour or three tons; the usual freight charged was one dollar per barrel, while the tolls between Philadelphia and Lancaster amounted to three dollars or about one dollar per ton.

Michaux, who traveled over the road in 1802, mentions that the taverns on the road were very numerous, and that the German language was spoken in almost all of them. He further says his fellow travelers were always thirsty, and would stop the stage at every tavern to drink some glasses of grog. This he states was a mixture of brandy and water, or rum and water, the proportions of which depended solely on the taste of each person.

Sutcliff, a public friend, mentions in his journal, 1806, 8th month 27th, "at the inn where I breakfasted, which was the General Paoli tavern, I met with a family who had landed a few days before in Philadelphia, and were now on their way to the Ohio. As they spoke neither English nor French, I was unable to make out from what part of the continent of Europe they came. The master of the inn informed me that he had reason to believe they had a very large property with them in the wagons in which they traveled."

As the traffic continued to increase the inn again soon became too small, and during the latter part of the first decade of the last century the large addition, 81 x 38 feet, facing the turnpike was built. It was completed in 1812, the year in which the second war with England was declared. After Governor Simon Snyder issued his proclamation, May 12, 1812, for volunteers, recruiting went on briskly at the Paoli as well as at the other taverns in the vicinity, the result of which was the mustering of the 97th Regiment, Pennsylvania Volunteers, into the service of the United States, May 5, 1813.

After the destruction of Washington by the British in 1814 great fears were entertained of an attempt to capture Philadelphia by way of Chester county. Another proclamation was issued by the Governor for the militia. Isaac Wayne, son of the General, was elected Colonel of the Second Regiment Volunteer Light Infantry, but it is said preferred to serve as a private soldier in a company of volunteer cavalry.

Joshua Evans continued to keep the house until April 23, 1814, when he was succeeded by his son Joshua Evans, jr. (born January, 1777), who soon became one of the most prominent and best known men in Chester county; he was a man of singular good sense and judgment, clear intellect, wonderful nerve, and was destined to exercise great power in both county and State; during his whole career he was an uncompromising Democrat of the Jefferson and Jackson school.

It does not appear what part he took, if any, in the war of 1812.

As an illustration of the great amount of travel at this early day it is but necessary to enumerate some of the land stages that passed and stopped at the house in 1814:

1. Baltimore Stage Turnpike Route via Lancaster every Second and Fourth days.
2. Carlisle stage.
3. Columbia stage.
4. Harrisburg Stage Line. Every day—Seventh-day only excepted—at 7 o'clock a. m. from the first of the Twelfth-month (December) to the fifteenth of Fourth-month (April) and five days in the week the remainder of the year. To proceed up the river from Harrisburg direct. Seats to be had on First-day (Sunday) at the stage office, corner High and Eighth streets.
5. The Pittsburg stage via Harrisburg.
6. The Lancaster stage. A daily line leaving High and Eighth streets at 7 o'clock in the morning.
7. York stage.
8. The Valley stage, from 164 High street.
9. West Chester stage, from No. 18 North Fourth street, Third, Fifth and Seventh days at 8 a. m.
10. Westtown School, from No. 80 High street every Fourth and Seventh days.

According to the postoffice regulations in 1812 mail stages were required to carry the mails from Philadelphia to Pittsburg in six ordinary days.

The arrival or departure of the stage coaches was always a matter of considerable excitement around the inn. As one would come thundering up or down the turnpike and draw up in front of the tavern, with its four fine horses prancing and covered with dust and foam, it would at once become the great center of interest. One of the hostlers would usually have the door of the coach open and be ready to assist the passengers to alight, even before the driver had time to come down from his seat, after throwing his reins to the ready stable boy. While the landlord and habitues of the barroom, the hostlers, stable boys and other hangers-on about the tavern yard would at once rush out, the former to welcome the travelers and possible guests, the latter prompted by idle curiosity, or in the hope of hearing scraps of the news or gossip of the day, as told by the drivers at the bar between " 'ere's to your good health," or while waiting for the relays to be substituted for the exhausted steeds. Then followed the embarking of the passengers, after their parting glass, the wishing of " God speed" by the host, the cracking of the driver's whip and on some lines the tooting of the horn, then the journey towards the next relay station commenced at full speed, where the same scenes would be re-enacted, and so on until the end of the journey would be reached. A traveler describing his stop at the Paoli in 1813 says: " A scene of bustle unprecedented by anything I had ever met before, presented itself till midnight, supper was three times spread for at least twenty people, and as the chambers were not very numerous we were under the necessity of agreeing amongst ourselves for bed fellows. My partner was a merchant with whose conversation I had been pleased during the evening and we were shown along the passages to a remote room. We were aroused at four o'clock in the morning to proceed on our journey to the city."

Another writer about the same period says: " At dusk when we stopped at the Paoli to water the horses and brandy the gentlemen the busy scene round the inn by the roadside with several great four-horse stages pouring forth their cargoes by the dozen would have furnished material for many a page in the sketch book, &c."

The following two advertisements in reference to the war of 1812 and the subject of this sketch appeared in the county paper under their respective dates:

March 16, 1816. I. Wynkop, regimental paymaster, advertises that he "will attend at the house of Joshua Evans, Paoli tavern, on Thursday, the fourth day of April next, to paying Captain Wersler's Company, Second Regt. Penn. Vol. Light Inf."

March 18, 1816. John G. Bull, paymaster of the 65th Pennsylvania Militia advertises that he "has appointed Tuesday, the 26th inst., at the Paoli in Tredyffrin township to meet Captain Campbel's company. Captain Weatherby's company on Wednesday, the 27th, at the same place."

During this year the "Republican Artillerists" were organized of which Joshua Evans at once became a prominent member.

Joshua Evans, the elder, died April 25, 1817. The reputation and prosperity of the Paoli continued to increase from year to year. As a result a number of taverns were established on the turnpike on both sides of the Paoli, the nearest one was the "General Jackson," just east of the Darby road. It was erected and presided over, as has been stated, by Randall Evans, a brother of Joshua. Tradition tells us that there were frequently outbursts of temper between the two brothers, as one would find the other interfering with his regular patrons. Joshua was elected to the State Legislature in 1820. At this period there were few pieces of property in the State outside of Philadelphia which were more valuable than the Paoli; the house was the gathering place for the surrounding townships, while the patronage from the travelers on the turnpike taxed the house to its fullest extent, so much so that there was very little show for a teamster or wagoner getting any accommodation. Among other enterprises of the proprietor was a large lumber yard on the turnpike east of the house.

In 1825 during Lafayette's visit to America Joshua Evans and Isaac Wayne were both on the committee which waited on the General for the purpose of inviting him to visit Chester county.

It was not until the following year, December 9, 1826, that a postoffice was established at the Paoli. Joshua Evans was appointed the first postmaster.

When, in 1826-7, the question of building the Columbia Railroad was being agitated it was urged by the friends of the enterprise, in furtherance of the project, that the prodigious advantage resulting from science may best be appreciated by reflecting that a weight, which, on an improved railroad, could be transported with facility by the agency of a single horse, would among our red brethren (who preceded us but a little over a century and a quarter) require the laborious application of a thousand "squaw" power to remove. In 1828 the Columbia Railroad was laid out and commenced by the Canal Commissioners of the State by order of an act of the Legislature of that year. This railroad, which is now a part of the great Pennsylvania Railroad system, was first surveyed under the direction of Major John Wilson, but was not finished until 1834. It is said that the first survey of the road was located from Columbia to the "Warren" without much difficulty, but from that point east great difficulties presented themselves, in finding a favorable route for leaving the Chester Valley. The route as run by Mr. Haines went through the valley from the Warren, north of the valley ridge, by way of Howelltown, recrossing to the south of the ridge a short distance north of the Spread Eagle Tavern; this route would have completely cut the Paoli off from the contemplated new highway.

The road was finally located on the south side of the valley ridge, so as to pass just north of the Paoli Tavern. It is said this conclusion was due to the influence and demands of General Evans, backed by several good dinners. In the meantime Evans had been elected to Congress, wherein he represented the District from 1829–33. The portion of the new road extending fourteen miles west from the "White Hall" was known as the Paoli section, and was constructed under the supervision of Enoch Davis. Following is a copy of the MSS. instructions issued to him for his guidance from the headquarters of the engineer corps at the Buck Tavern.

Instructions to Superintendents.

It will be the duty of the superintendent to see that the stakes set by the assistant engineers are preserved and that the trenches are laid out agreeably to the directions. He will examine the length, depth and width of the trenches, and in no case shall any trench be filled in with broken stone, before it has been examined by the superintendent or before the broken stone has been inspected by the assistant engineer.

The superintendent will attend particularly to the examining of the broken stone, as expressed in the printed specifications.

He will inspect the sleepers as they are distributed on the road, and will suffer none to be laid which he does not consider in conformity to the specifications, taking however, the earliest opportunity to report to the assistant engineer having charge of the work, any materials which he may reject.

The superintendent will see that the sleepers are properly bedded and rammed and that the work is executed strictly according to the specifications.

If any directions given by the superintendent are disregarded, he will immediately report to the assistant engineer.

It will be the duty of the superintendent to report all defective work without delay.

E. Div. Colm. & Phila. Railway.

September, 1832.

Specifications for Laying Wooden Rails, Sills.

The wooden sills shall be of chestnut, chestnut oak or white oak free from sap and sound in every respect, seven and a half feet in length, and of sufficient size to square seven inches. They will be dressed flat on the under side-and notched out on the upper side for the horse path and for the reception of the string pieces according to the plan and directions of the engineer.

Trenches.

The trenches for the reception of the broken stone shall be four feet apart from centre to centre, one foot in width, sixteen inches in depth and eight feet in length; where the trench is cut in rock the depth need not exceed four inches. The earth excavated from the trenches must be removed from the graded surface of the road and deposited on the slopes of the nearest embankment, the same will be done with the earth taken from the surface of such embankments as may be required to be reduced to the proper grade.

Broken Stone.

The stone upon which the sills are to be bedded, no particle of which must be larger than a cube of two inches, must be approved by the engineer before being used.   No earth, no clay or material must be suffered to be mixed with the broken stone.

Layings.

The position, vertical and horizontal, of the track will be given at convenient distances by the Engineer; the contractor completing the levels and curvatures required.

The width and depth of the trenches having been formed as above mentioned, broken stone to the depth of four inches will be put in, and well compacted with a heavy rammer; more may then be added, but in no case shall more than four inches be put in without being thus compacted.

The sills may now be laid, and firmly adjusted to the proper level with a wooden rammer; the string pieces can be placed in the notches, and keyed up; the inner edges chamfered off one inch, and the iron base put agreeably to the directions of the engineer.   The broken stone will then be placed on the horsepath so that the track may be finished for use.

The keys may be of white oak or yellow pine, one foot in length, two inches in height, and one and a half inches thick, tapering to three-quarters.   It is expected that every part of the work will be executed in a faithful and workmanship manner; no indifferent or careless work will be estimated or received.

As will be seen by above specifications the railway of eighty years ago was entirely different from the present magnificent highway, with its quadruple tracks, and elaborate system of automatic switches and block signals; the railway as first constructed consisted of a single track formed partly of stone sills, and partly of wooden rails, plated with flat bars of iron.   The space between the rails being filled in with broken stone for the horses to travel on, as the rails were but a small distance above the horse track, the consequence was that pieces of the "stuffing" were continually coming in contact with the wheels to the great disadvantage of the draught. Another serious difficulty which presented itself, while the road was run by horse power upon the highway principle, was the regulating of the speed of the different trains. It is well known that scarcely two teams can be found to propel the same weight with equal speed, and that a horse when loaded should not travel faster than two and one half miles per hour to produce this maximum effect, while the passenger cars were expected to make about eight miles an hour if they were to supersede the "Land Stages" on the Turnpike. Another great obstacle in the way of uniform speed was the constantly varying grade of the Columbia railroad; a fact which further enhanced the difficulty in proportion to the increased length of road traveled, the power of the horses being constantly impaired by the fatigue of their muscles made frequent relays necessary. Consequently, the attempt to make all cars travel at a uniform rate of speed proved an absolute failure from the start.

The first car passed over the new road October 18, 1832, from Belmont to the West Chester intersection (Malvern). It carried the United States mail and thirty passengers, and was drawn by two horses. It took the place of the Lancaster mail coach between these points. It was not until Christmas, 1833, that the first car passed from Broad and Vine streets to West Chester.

These early cars were small four wheel affairs, somewhat like the present "Tally-ho" four-in-hand coaches. They were drawn by two horses tandem, and known as "Fly Coaches" or "Fire Flies." Seats for passengers were arranged inside as well as outside on the top of the car, with a seat for the driver at each end of the car.

These cars remained in use for several years. A short time after steam became the motive power they were abandoned as the smoke and sparks from the engine made it impossible for passengers to ride with comfort on top of the cars.

One of the first rules issued to the collectors under date of February 6, 1834, reads: "You are hereby informed that the proprietors or agents of cars will not be allowed to use two horses abreast upon the Columbia and Philadelphia Railway. This method of propelling cars is injurious to the railway and you will therefore consider it a part of your duty to enforce the law in case the above rule should be violated. Signed, EDW. J. GRAY, Engineer."

From the official report to the Legislature we find that from Oct. 18 to Nov. 2, 1832, thirteen hundred and twenty-two passengers were transported over the road.

The Paoli now became the terminus of the Pittsburg stage coaches, the travelers being taken to and from Philadelphia on the horse cars on the railroad; this lasted but for a short time as, on account of the rivarly between the two brothers, it was found necessary by the proprietors of the coach line to remove their terminus to the Green Tree tavern, about one mile further west. Turnouts were located at convenient points and "half-way posts" were planted between every two turnouts, the regulation being that when two cars from opposite directions came on the section the car passing the half-way post first had the right of way, the other cars on the section having to hitch their horses to the rear end of the car and retrace their steps and pull on to the next turnout. This matter gave rise to considerable trouble between the opposing drivers, and in November, 1834, caused a serious accident to two passenger cars, just west of Paoli. It was about noon when two cars were approaching each other, with great speed on the same tracks, the post being between them. As they approached that point, the horses were lashed for the victory, and though as they approached each other, the brakes were put down, it was impossible to stop them. The horses sprang aside and the cars came together with tremendous force, breaking in their fronts and strongest timbers, producing the utmost consternation and distress among the passengers, and seriously wounding such as were most exposed. One gentleman sitting on the driver's seat received the opposite car against his knee, and was probably seriously hurt. The Rev. Dr. Neil received a violent blow upon his head, which seriously affected him through the day. The wounded passengers were taken to Philadelphia in another car.

Although the building of the railroad eventually had a disastrous effect upon the turnpike hostelries, it was different with the Paoli; the tact and influence of General Evans was exerted to so great an extent, as to make the inn one of the most important stopping places on the new highway; as well as having the office of the first toll collector west of Philadelphia located here. This building, still standing, is the house just east of the railroad bridge, directly back of the present Paoli station. Consequently at the meeting of the Canal Commissioners held at Harrisburg, March 12, 1834, "Enoch Davis was unanimously appointed collector upon the Columbia railway at the Paoli"; further ordered that he shall be allowed fifty dollars per month as a full compensation for his services, and that as soon as weigh scales are completed at his office, he perform the duties of weigh master, and weigh all burden cars using said railway. A postscript on his commission from

the Governor reads: "Present me kindly to my friend
General Evans when you see him."

From the official "Rates of Toll" we learn that the
charges for use of the road were:

On each burden car per mile,	1 cent	0 mills.
do do passenger car per mile,	2 do	0 do.
do do baggage car per mile,	2 do	0 do.
do on each passenger over 12 years of age, transported in a car, of any description, per mile,	1 do	0 do.
On each passenger between 6 and 12 years of age, per mile,	0 do	5 do.
All freight was charged at so much per 1000 lbs per mile, usually from 5 mills to two cents per mile.		

Davis remained in office until March, 1836, during
which time the tolls and fines collected by him at Paoli
amounted to $16,454.73; fines and treble tolls constitute
quite an item in the above amount.

John Williams, John Rowan and Isaac Powell were
successively appointed as "Collectors of tolls and fines"
for the State at this point.

It was not long before General Evans constructed a
private siding at the Paoli and urged his neighbors to use
the road as a means of taking their products to market.
Other parties along the line were not slow in following the
example set by General Evans, and in a short time there
were over twenty private sidings between the Paoli and
the inclined plane at Belmont. But after a short trial it
was found that nothing was more detrimental to the reputation of the experimental road than this indiscriminate
use of the highway by the inhabitants residing along the
line; the multitude of small cars, the horses traveling at a

degree of speed to suit the driver, soon caused so many vexatious delays as to make the road almost useless for passenger travel.

For several years both horse and steam power were used. This led to numerous complications, accidents and collisions, and as the road continued to grow in popularity with all parties, it was soon manifest that steam would have to supplant horse power at an early date, so the south track was relaid with cross ties and T-rails for the use of locomotives, while the individual cars drawn by horses were relegated to the north track with its granite blocks and wooden sills. It was not until after 1840 that locomotives became the exclusive motive power.

General Evans, at the first introduction of steam, had a wood and water station located on his property near the tavern. This was no sooner done than Randall in opposition to Joshua erected a large water tank for the use of the engines on the railroad just back of his inn the "General Jackson." This caused the rivalry between the two brothers to break out again with all the rancor of old; however, Randall's efforts seemed futile as Joshua carried the day.

Wood at that early day was the only fuel used for the locomotives. After the establishment of this depot, the farmers soon found a lucrative business in supplying the State with cord wood during their dull season; the yard also gave employment to a number of wood sawyers. Queer tales are still current in the vicinity about some old stumps and logs which it appears were regularly corded over and over again at the expense of the State by the favored few who were in the ring. All trains stopped to "wood up" as well as to take in water; on such occasions both passengers and crew would go into the inn for lunch and refreshments.

During the latter part of Gen. Evans's time the Paoli was also the polling place for the five adjoining townships, viz.:

Tredyffrin, Easttown, East Whiteland, Willistown and Charlestown. It was not an uncommon occurrence for over five hundred persons to be in and about the inn on an election day, while on the day of a grand " Democratic Rally " the horses and vehicles could be counted by the hundreds and the attendants by the thousands. The American flag with its twenty-six stars, used at the Paoli, during the two Jackson campaigns was still in good condition not many years ago and was unfurled during recent campaigns in Tredyffrin. Large sales and vendues were also frequently cried at the inn.

Shortly before the death of General Evans, in 1846, the, patronage by way of the railroad increased to so great an extent as to necessitate the erection of a separate barroom to accommodate the traveling public. While the inn proper became known as a favorite summer resort and boarding house, some of Philadelphia's most prominent citizens spending the summer there year after year.

The new building was erected facing the railroad, where the Valley road formerly crossed at grade. It had two stories and porches in the front and rear; the upper room was used for meetings and parties, while the lower room was used as a bar and lunch room, the bar extended along the south and west side of the room. The latter was devoted to the postoffice and the sale of liquors. The wall back of the bar was laid out in three panels with a large full length figure of Shakespeare and Milton in the two end panels. The counter on the south side was used for

JOHN D. EVANS.

THE LAST PROPRIETOR OF THE "PAOLI".

lunch and coffee. Whenever a train arrived, at the call of the train hands of "all out, five minutes for refreshments," the passengers would rush to the bar, through the four large doors facing the track, until the room was packed, but even those within reach of the counter would hardly have time to gulp down their coffee and doughnut or sandwich before the bell would ring and the train start at the command "all aboard," while the passengers were left to scramble into the cars with their luncheon in their hands as best they were able.

One of the earliest recollections the writer has of this barroom is watching the mechanics while covering the floor with a heavy sheet of zinc, fastened down with large brass headed nails. The large egg-shaped stove stood in a box of sand in the center of the floor, while in a circle around the stove there was formed by driving nails through large copper cents of the period, in large capitals, the well known watchword of "Mad Anthony," "REMEMBER PAOLI!"

When John D. Evans succeeded to the ownership of the inn at the death of his father, the activity and bustle at the Paoli was probably not equaled at any similar establishment in the State.

Previous to 1836, when steam supplanted the uncertain horse-power, the second track had been completed and the new road continued to grow in public favor and it soon became a part of the system (in fact) of communication between Philadelphia and Pittsburgh, in connection with the State canals. The boats used on the canals for carrying both freight and passengers were built in three or four sections; these sections were floated on or off the trucks at the respective termini of the railroad. It was a curious sight to see a locomotive drawing a train of these sections,

the bodies of which were invariably painted white, while
the cabin windows were hung with Turkey red curtains
and could be closed with green slat shutters.

After the sale of the State improvements to the Pennsylvania Railroad Co. by the State in 1855, Paoli was
made the terminus for local trains, an engine house and
turntable were built a little northwest of the station for
the purpose of turning an entire train.

The cottage resident who now goes daily over the present magnificent road on the Paoli or Bryn Mawr express
in a little over thirty minutes, from Paoli to the city, can
little picture to himself the first local trains, or how we
rejoiced at the two hour schedule to and from the city,
and when shortly after the war the time from 31st and
Market to Paoli was reduced to one and a half hours, we
thought the utmost rate of speed had been attained; also
how some of the more timid passengers shook their heads
and complained to the conductors about the reckless speed
of the two Paoli trains as they would swing around the
old double curves between the Eagle and Paoli. When
chain brakes were first tried on the locomotives in 1870,
even some of the brakemen refused to go on the trains so
equipped and were transferred to other trains, where the
"Iron" was yet twisted by hand. The early commutation
ticket was a somewhat different affair from the present
handy three months' folder. The fact was when bought at
the first of the month the ticket was a string of coupons
over four feet long, and the coupon was no good unless
detached by the conductor.

One of the best known characters usually to be found
at the Paoli, when not on the local trains, was a half-breed
Indian "Theodore Plumbly"; he was the first person to
regularly supply travelers on the road, or residents along

the line, with Philadelphia newspapers on the morning of the day on which they were published. Plumbly was well known to all regular riders. His tall spare figure, dark eyes, prominent features and jet black hair always worn in a roll turned up over his collar, will be easily recalled by anyone who ever saw him. In some things he was very eccentric; if he took a dislike to a person no money could induce him to supply that person with a paper. His feet and hands were exceedingly small, and he was known far and near for his agility. The writer has frequently seen him jump on or off an express train while going at full speed around the old curve at Paoli; he would seem to leap up in the air before alighting on his feet; frequently he would have a large bundle of papers under his arm at the time. Plumbly was also an expert runner; his boast was that he could beat any horse into the city from Paoli. If he missed a morning train, which was frequently the case, more especially on Sundays, he would think nothing of starting up the pike, deliver his papers occasionally as far as Downingtown, and trot back to the Paoli, where he would spend the balance of the afternoon. Plumbly died October 29, 1878.

During the Centennial year the old inn yard and stables were once more crowded, more so than they had been for many a year. On some days there would be almost two hundred vehicles left there. Still nothing worthy of special mention occurred at the Paoli until the week following Sunday, July 22, 1877, when the railroad riots broke out in Pittsburgh. A number of hands were working on the road at this point, and threats were soon made against the company's property. However, the firm action and counsels of a few prominent residents together with the encampment of the "Washington Troop" in the vicinity nipped the incipient riot in the bud.   On September 21 of this year the centennial anniversary of the massacre took place on the grounds.   The residents of Tredyffrin and Easttown assembled at the inn in the morning and marched to the grounds.   The Easttown deputation was mounted and carried a banner inscribed "Easttown, the birthplace of Gen. Wayne."

Soon afterwards the roadbed of the railway was changed further to the north, where it now is.   This cut the old inn as well as the barroom and eating station off from the road.   A new station was built below the signal tower, and the grade of the Valley road raised so as to cross the tracks by a bridge and thus obviate the former dangerous grade crossing.

Shortly after these changes were made, John D. Evans removed to the old Jackson or Evenson property.   He lived here until his death, June 6, 1883.   In 1881 he sold the balance of the tract containing the old Paoli and 350 acres to a party of gentlemen from Philadelphia, known as the "Paoli Improvement Company," by whom the tract was laid out into building lots and advertised for sale.

The old inn after an existence of over a century as a favorite public house of entertainment for man and beast, noted far and wide for its good cheer, was now remodeled and the old inn-yard fenced in to make it answer for a so-called fashionable resort of the present day.

However, none of the parties who have engaged in the venture, have been able to make a paying success out of the new departure, and the old inn at the present writing (1886) is closed, without an occupant, and in place of the former scenes of life and activity, quiet and desolation now reign supreme; the closed house and the deserted grounds, repelling rather than attracting the passer by.   Whether a tenant will be found who will succeed in even temporarily galvanizing the old hostelry back into life is a question that time alone can tell; but it is exceedingly doubtful if anything approximating the past reputation of the old Paoli will ever be reached under the present régime.[2]

The inn property has also changed ownership as well as landlords several times since the sale to the Improvement Company.

Since the turnpike has again been put in first-class condition, and is now known as Lancaster avenue from Philadelphia to Paoli, Paoli had become the goal of the wheelmen's club, and during the time that bicycling was in vogue there were often over fifty "wheels" of all kinds and construction to be seen leaning against the fence now enclosing the old tavern yard, while the owners were regaling themselves in or about the old farm house between the inn and the present railroad station previous to their spin back to the city along the smooth road leading through the numerous suburban hamlets which now line that thoroughfare.

---

[2] A few years later the old landmark was destroyed by fire.

THE "GREEN TREE" IN WILLISTOWN TOWNSHIP.

A FEW days after the occurrence chronicled in the previous chapter on the old "Ship," the sun printer armed with note book and sharpened pencils in addition to some specimen blue prints of familiar landmarks on the old turnpike, sought out the old resident. He of the "Old Hickory Club" who a few days ago had so kindly offered to shake out the folds of his memory, sweep away the cobwebs of time, thus lifting the veil from the past and conjure up scenes of the bygone time as recollected by him, vague, shadowy and oft incoherent though they might be, still would prove as instructive and interesting a revelation to the inquisitive quasi historian as a lantern journey through a foreign clime does to the studious schoolboy.

On entering the humble abode the writer at once saw

and felt that he was welcome. Before his footstep had crossed the sill he was met by his loquacious acquaintance with a hearty "Why, how do you do Mister; glad to see you agin; come right in; feared I talked you so tired the other day that you wouldn't want to meet me again, but walk right in; have a glass of whisky; no; well it's true, 'tisn't like the widow Evans' used to be, but it's the best I can get around here. Miranda, come here a minute. This is the picture man I was telling you about taking pictures of the old taverns on the pike. Miranda is my wife, Mister. Her father used to be a teamster on the old road and made many a trip between Columbia and Philadelphia. He used to haul flour one way and store goods the other." With this introduction the wife approached and greeted the visitor: "Yes, the old man has been telling me about you; I scolded him for telling such things to strangers and told him he ought to know better, but he is getting old and likes to talk. He keeps saying 'the times is all wrong'; that if the 'Old Hickory Club' was still about, with plenty of old time whisky, things would be different, but, Mister, don't get offended at anything he says; he is a good man, if he is old; and still votes for Jackson, as he says, at every election. He can't get Old Hickory out of his head. Why when the war broke out in '61 he came home one day and says: 'Mirandy, I've gone and 'listed.' Good gracious, says I, are you gone crazy as old as you are. 'Well,' says he, 'you recollect the Old Hickory Club I belonged to afore we was married; well our motto was Andy Jackson's orders: 'The Union must and shall be preserved.' So away he went, the Regiment was the 97th; you've heard of it, I suppose; it was the Chester county regiment. Well he came home with what was left of them, but he was pretty well used up." Here the husband interrupted his wife and told her she had better not talk so much.   In the meantime the amateur had taken out his blue prints, and handed them to both Miranda and her husband, who carefully examined them, holding the views at arm's length to suit the focus of his failing eyes, while his wife wiped and adjusted her spectacles.   After a few seconds he broke the silence: "So they are the pictures you took the other day; well, if the widow Evans or any of the jolly stage drivers, who used to stop there, was to come back and see this, they would never know it for the old 'Ship.'   The picture is all right, Mister, as it is now, but not as it used to be.   Mirandy, go tend to your dinner. Now, Mister, we are alone.   These women will talk, seems to come natural to them; they will talk, they can't help it.   How long have our folks lived around here? Well, Mister, let me see.   I can't exactly tell; but my grandfather's father was out with Colonel Bouquet again the French; my grandfather was under Colonel Humpton at Paoli, and was drilled by General Steuben at Valley Forge; know where that is, I reckon.   I suppose you heard of the Paoli fight, haven't ye?   Well the old man got off; hid in the swamp all night, but reported in Downingtown before noon the next day.   Did I ever hear him tell about that night?   No, he was dead before I was born, but 'pap' often told us boys all about it, but it's so long ago I almost forget.   You would like to know what I heard. Well, I will try and think about it some time.   Excuse me, Mister, ain't you dry?"   "No."   "Well, I am."   On the old man's return, after a few moments absence, he continued: "My father fought in 1812 under Colonel Cromwell Pearce; ever heard of him?   Well, he is buried over there in the valley.   He was a great man in the county when I was a boy, and many a time I heard 'pap' and the Colonel talking over about old times, when I was a boy.

"Mirandy; well, her folks was Welsh. A whole ship-load of first cousins came over all at one time way back in Penn's time. Her father used to team along the pike, as I told you afore. I often heard him say, that after the war of 1812 there were several thousand wagons continually on the road between Philadelphia and Pittsburgh. 'Pitt Teams' we called them for short; they were longer and heavier than the Conestogas that went to Columbia. Most of these 'Pitt Teams' were drawn by six or eight horses and were loaded up from sixty to eighty hundred weight, and they traveled from 18 to 22 miles a day, making the round trip, between Philadelphia and Pittsburgh, in from 30 to 35 days. They always went in squads of half a dozen to thirty in a string, and kept company for the whole distance; this was for protection as well as company, as highwaymen and thieves were not the least fear of the plodding teamster.

"These 'strings,' as they were called, had their regular 'stands' to stay over night, and it was not an unusual sight for fifty to sixty of these teams to meet at one stand for rest.

"The drivers carried a mattress and quilt or blanket, and after they had fed themselves, and their horses, and drunk their usual potation of whiskey, they spread the mattress on the floor of the barroom, and went to sleep amid the turmoil of the barroom; such was the only bed on which many of these hardy teamsters slept from one year's end to another, never undressing, except merely to take off their coats, it was an exception for any of this class to change any part of his clothing from one end of the journey to the other. So you see, Mister, we are native stock, both of us—Miranda and I. Hope you are not getting out of patience. Well, speaking about the pike above Paoli, did

you ever hear of the 'Green Tree'?   Well, after leaving
Paoli, now as you come up the pike, the first improvement
you come to is a little church near the top of the hill.   It
is the 'Mission of the Good Samaritan at Paoli.'   This
church was built in the centennial year by an old gentleman,
as a memorial for his wife, who for some twenty years
boarded at the 'Paoli.'   A little further on at the cross-
roads, you see an old shop.   This used to be the Thomas'
shops; were built in 1812 and did a big business in turnpike
days.   Thomas, who built them, was no relation to the
Valley Thomas', but came from Canada, with the 'soldiers' and settled here.

"A little further west, at the next road crossing near the
19th milestone, is where the 'Green Tree' stood.   It is in
Willistown township and here the Grubb's mill road crosses
the turnpike, the latter having ascended the South Valley
hill, commences to dip into the 'Great Valley.'   Why do
they call it the Great Valley?   Well, I asked that once
when I was a schoolboy and the master told me the right
name was the 'Great Limestone Valley,' but the name was
long, so in the course of time the middle name was dropped
This explains it; but as I was saying about the 'Green
Tree,' when I was a youngster that tavern was a busy
spot."   We will here leave the old resident for a short
time and devote it to the history of the

GREEN TREE IN WILLISTOWN.

The inn was known as a wagon stand, and in appearance
was similar to the taverns of the time, viz: two stories
high, capped by a high attic, porch in front and side, with
pump and trough in the tavern yard in front of the house
for the convenience of travelers and drovers.   The old inn
when built shortly after the revolution stood on the old

Lancaster road, same as the Blue Ball, Bear and Admiral Warren. George King is said to have been the builder and host of the first house. He died in 1792. Then Isaac King succeeded to the ownership. It was during his term that the turnpike was built, and fortunately for the tavern keeper the road at this point was laid out to run over or near the old roadbed.

As soon as the new highway was completed Isaac King turned the property over to Abram and Joseph King. This was in April, 1797. They kept the house jointly until April 1, 1805, when Joseph King deeded his share and interest to Abram. The house had prospered as travel increased, and the large tree, with wide-spreading branches clothed in full foliage, painted on the swinging signboard which hung in its yoke at the top of a high pole, became one of the best-known landmarks to the toiler on the highway.

Abram King now enlarged the capacity of the house and made many improvements, not the least of which was the building of the large farm barn and stables (demolished 1888). High up in the gable was the legend—A. K. E. —1805. Another curious object about this barn was a large oblong cornerstone in the front or south side, high up in the wall, just below the eaves. This stone bore the legend "24" in antique figures. It was a sandstone, the rest of the stones used in the building being the blue limestone or marble of the Valley.

This marked stone was nothing more nor less than one of the milestones of the first road, which followed the old Indian trail, through the wilderness, from the Schuylkill to the Brandywine. The inscription 24 meant that it was twenty-four miles from the Court House in Philadelphia, at Second and Market streets, to that point by way of the public road.   The stone, however, did not long remain a true prophet to the wayfarer, as, when the Lancaster road was ordered to be laid out by the Provincial Council, the road was straightened so as to shorten the distance between the old stone and the city almost two miles.   When afterwards the turnpike was constructed, more kinks were taken out, and the new stone bore the legend 19 to Phila., which was equal to 21 miles to Second and Market Streets.

So when Abram King built his barn, in 1805, the old useless milestone was utilized as a cornerstone, and remained there, a veritable landmark of the past, unknown and forgotten, until just before the barn was demolished, when by the merest accident it was discovered, saved from the rubbish, and by courtesy of ex-Sheriff Gill, the owner, presented to the writer.

Abram King in 1816 passed the title to George and Joseph King, presumably brothers.   A few years later the King family, however, seem to have gotten into financial difficulty, and the whole property—farm, tavern and all— was seized and sold Aug. 1, 1820 by Sampson Babb, Esq., High Sheriff of Chester County, to Abram Phillips, after having been in the possession of the King family about sixty years.   Before the month of August had expired Phillips sold the inn to Henry Coffman, who was of German descent, and is said to have been raised over on the North Valley Hill.   Be this as it may, Henry Coffman and his wife, Catherine, knew how to keep a hotel, and it was not long before the tavern yard was nightly crowded with wagoners' teams of all descriptions, while the barroom was filled with Pennsylvania Dutch teamsters.   The Green Tree also became the stopping place for the Mennonites and Amish who traveled along the road, as Coffman was himself a member of the Mennonite community in the

AYMISH MENNONITES OF LANCASTER COUNTY.

Valleys, and always wore plain clothes with large hooks and eyes in place of buttons, after the manner of the more strict branch of the Amish. The inn was the first public house west of Philadelphia, kept by a "Hooker" Mennonite. This fact alone insured the house a large, if not remunerative, patronage.

Henry Coffman further was an especial favorite with the Pittsburgh wagoners, of whose habits mention has already been made.

This hardy class of men brought forth by the times in which they lived, formed a clan, as it were, by themselves, the same as the Lancaster county Germans, and became particularly fitted for their occupation. The majority of this class were honest, industrious and trustworthy, and noted for their endurance; although all were addicted to the constant use of whiskey, they rarely became under its baneful influence, so as to interfere with their vocation.

There were exceptions to this rule, however, examples of which were given in previous articles on the old inns.

The regular Pittsburgh wagoners would rise early to feed and clean their horses. As soon as they had their breakfast and harnessed their horses they would start on their journey and would not stop to feed themselves or their teams until they arrived at the wagon stand, which was to form the end of their day's route, the only exception or break to their tiresome tour being their stops at the wayside inns to water their horses and liquor themselves.

They ate but two regular meals a day, for each of which they paid twenty-two cents. Their horses were fed oats and rye, which they purchased from the tavern keeper at a few cents advance on the original cost. The first cost of their meals was more than the tavern keeper received from them, consequently the only profit the host of a wagon stand made from his customers was that which arose from the sale of his whiskey and the manure in his yard. Many of these teams perhaps never saw the inside of a barn or shed during their lives.

At night the harness was taken off and laid on the guide pole connecting the two axletrees and protruding out back of the wagon. The horses were tied to different parts of the wagon and fed from feed troughs, which were carried for that purpose on the journey, and no matter how inclement the weather the poor beasts were forced to stand in the open air without shelter and at the mercy of the elements.

Frequently kind-hearted travelers, strangers to the customs of the turnpike, would ask a wagoner why he did not put his horses into the stable during the storm? The reply would always be "that they do better by standing out," and in proof of the truth of their assertion they would challenge their questioner to show them a single poor horse among the many thousands that were harnessed in the "Pitt Teams" on the turnpike.

The wages of these teamsters was usually from eight to ten dollars a month. Small as this amount seems at the present day, yet by thrift and frugality they were able to save enough out of this pittance to purchase within a year or two a wagon and a team of their own.

There were also cases where some of these wagoners became quite wealthy and had a dozen or more teams on the road. In some cases they would start their teams out in a string, while they would accompany them on horseback and after delivering their freight in Pittsburgh would purchase flour and whisky, load their teams, transport it East and sell the cargo on their own account.

Nothing of particular interest occurred during the next

few years of Henry Coffman's regime, until about 1826, when the new State Railroad from Philadelphia to Columbia was projected. At first came vague rumors. These were soon followed by information that the new enterprise was a fact. Then came the corps of engineers under the immediate supervision of Samuel Haines, the City Surveyor of Philadelphia. Coffman opposed and denounced the new project. Still, as the road as first laid out did not come near the "Green Tree," his opposition was expended in ridiculing the enterprise in choice Pennsylvania Dutch whenever the opportunity offered.

It may be of interest to some of the present residents of the vicinity to know where the surveys of the railroad were originally run, viz:

From the summit near the White Horse Inn, in West Whiteland, the line crossed the valley in a southern direction towards Kennard's School House (near the Steamboat Inn). It then continued on the north side of the turnpike to the ridge near the Chester County Academy; here the line crossed the turnpike and kept to the south of it along the face of South Valley Hill past the Warren, until the toll-gate near the 20th milestone was reached; this was just east of the Warren Tavern, then the line crossed the turnpike, and continued on the course until about north of the Paoli, when the line was run down the Valley by way of Davis' Tavern (Howellville) and thence through a ravine above the Spread Eagle Tavern, five miles below the Green Tree. As will be seen had this route been adopted it would have left all the tavern stands between the Warren and Spread Eagle isolated—cut off from the highways of travel.

The means taken by General Evans to induce the engineers to change this route, have been given in a previous article.   John Wilson, chief engineer, in his report to the Canal Commissioners, gives as a reason for changing the route to where it was afterwards built " we proceeded with the location of the railway eastward, in a direction toward the Green Tree Tavern, for the purpose of keeping open the ridge dividing the waters of the ' Valley' and Crum Creek, etc."   In his estimate he mentions the sixty first mile from Columbia as being traced along the summit of the valley ridge on favorable ground, crossing one small ravine near "Dempsey's," the line passing between the Green Tree tavern and barn, the mile ending on the north edge of the turnpike, etc.

This was afterward modified so the line was just north of the inn.   The turnpike at the west end of the tavern lot curved sharply to the north in its course down the slope of the valley hill, crossing the railroad at grade.   This crossing in after years proved to be one of the most dangerous in the county.

When Coffman first heard of this contemplated change of route, he gave the rumor no credence, but when the engineer corps came and finally located the route between the house and barn, and entangled the lines so that it was hard to tell which was the railroad or the turnpike, his anger now knew no bounds.   He declared that the new Riegle-weg was merely a scheme of the "Teufel" which had been conceived and hatched out in the Freemasons Lodges; it is almost needless to say that our Pennsylvania German was in thorough accord with the most radical "Anti" in the county.   He lost no opportunity to vent his spleen against both institutions, which he always coupled together; he went so far as to refuse under any circumstances to harbor or shelter at his house any one connected with the new State improvement, and woe to the luckless railroad man, of whatever grade, who through ignorance or foolhardiness entered the house in quest of the coveted glass of whiskey. If Coffman saw and recognized the visitor the latter was sure to get a torrent of abuse in choice "Hooker Dutch" about "Riegelwegs or Teufels bahn" in general, himself in particular, and a tirade ending with an order to get "Schnell araus," but no whiskey.

Still the innkeeper kept consoling himself with the idea that, on account of his opposition to the improvement, the new road would never be built, however, as the work progressed his phlegmatic Teuton blood was still further aroused, so much so that he solemnly declared that if the Teufels bahn was built he would sell out and go away, no matter what became of the wagoners or the country. Notwithstanding Coffman's threats the contractors laid their wooden sills and iron plates. The innkeeper, seeing that his opposition amounted to nothing, put his threat into execution and sold the property early in 1832 to Jonathan Jones, of Honeybrook, late High Sheriff, 1825–8, who took possession April 1st, 1832. It is said that Catherine Coffman was also of a thrifty turn and when it came to her time to sign the title papers absolutely refused to attach her signature unless a fine black silk dress was first given her, exclusive of the consideration mentioned in the deed.

A peculiarity about the Green Tree, during Coffman's ownership, was the large number of fine chickens he raised. These fowls were his stand-by in case guests arrived who wanted a meal different from the usual wagoner's fare. In such a case he would take a handful of corn, go out in the tavern yard, call his chickens around him, and, throwing them a few grains of corn, he would dexterously knock over with the short cane he usually carried as many of the fowls as were wanted for the meal.

After his retirement from the inn he bought and moved on a farm in East Whiteland, near the White Horse tavern, where he lived until he died.

With the advent of Jonathan Jones as host of the "Green Tree" the old tavern stand entered upon a new period of popularity. The house under the new proprietor, who for several years had presided over the well known "Boot" in Goshen, lost none of its renown as a wagon stand, while in his attitude towards the new railroad, which was now nearing completion, Jones from the first adopted a policy diametrically opposite to that pursued by his predecessor, and calculated to attract the patronage of those who were engaged in the new enterprise. It was not long before the cars were run on the new road. The passenger cars were small concerns, somewhat like a stage coach, and were drawn by two horses tandem, travelling between the rails. They were known as "fire-flies" on account of their bright red color. At first they were run as far as the "Gen. Paoli," where the passengers were transferred to the regular stage coach. This arrangement was no sooner started than the old wrangle broke out between the two rival Evans' at Paoli. The result of this was that the terminus of the new road was changed as speedily as possible to the Green Tree, a turntable put in, and the house made the transfer station of the mail and passengers for the time being.

The house for some time previous had been the terminus of the West Chester Railroad. William Williamson, the Secretary of the last named road, under date of October 23d, 1832, gave public notice that "until further notice the cars would leave West Chester at 8 a. m. and 2 p. m., and in return leave the house of Jonathan Jones at the Green Tree tavern at 10 a. m. and 4 p. m. Further that as soon as the Pennsylvania Railroad is finished the trains will be run to Paoli, leaving 20 minutes sooner." How, in the course of time, the road grew in the popular favor, and the turnpike travel declined, how the uncertain horse power was gradually superseded by steam power, after the successful trip of the "Black Hawk," April 16, 1834, has been set forth in a previous chapter, and need not be retold here. The first passenger cars carried passengers on the outside as well as inside, and the primitive locomotive drew three or four of these small cars in a train. The first serious accident which happened on a steam train in the vicinity occurred July 11, 1835. As the train was a short distance from Paoli, and passing under an apple tree, Patrick Daily, an outside passenger, stood up and reached out for an apple. An overhanging limb knocked his hat off, and in his efforts to regain the hat, lost his balance and fell under the wheels of the car, the whole train passing over his right leg. Daily was at once carried to a neighboring house and a doctor summoned, who on his arrival was so appalled at the sight of the mutilated limb that he could do nothing for the sufferer but advise his removal to the Pennsylvania Hospital, which was done as soon as a car could be gotten ready for the purpose. It is needless to say that in the meantime the patient bled to death.

From the completion of the road by the favorable location of the inn, together with the tact of Jones, the Green Tree from the start became a regular stopping station for trains and travelers over the new road.

Jonathan Jones, was also an enthusiastic Free Mason, who had come through an anti-Masonic storm unscathed, and it may not be amiss here to state that his "clothing" and jewels are to the present day prized as precious heir-

looms by his descendants.   The house soon became the
rallying point for the brethren of the vicinity; the meetings
were held in an upper room of the old inn, and by a curious
coincidence each visitor before he entered would give three
low, distinct knocks on the door which were answered from
within.   While on the table there would be a copy of Holy
Writ, and three lighted candles—always sure to be in the
same position.   It also happened that a plain Masonic
emblem could be seen lying on the sacred volume; possibly
this happened by accident.   The jewel might have fallen
out of the pocket of some one present as he reached over
the table to snuff one of the candles.   Be this as it may, on
these occasions the proscribed emblems were always to be
found resting on the open pages.

Thus these few homeless brethren, who though reviled
and persecuted, still kept alive some show of an organization, true to the precepts of the ancient Order.   Here,
under this friendly roof, they met unsuspected and in
safety; while oft perhaps in the bar below a parcel of
rabid "Anti's" between their cups and brawls, would be
denouncing the Order in general, breathing vengeance to
all its votaries, and congratulating themselves that the
hated institution had been broken up and scattered; little
thinking that above them under the same roof tree, there
were brethren good and true, who met for the purpose of
keeping alive the traditions and teachings of the maligned
Order, and anxiously longing for the time to come when
the clouds of intolerance would be dispelled, and the bright
sun of charity again shed its benign light over our land,
and they be enabled to once more organize as a Lodge.

Among the curious characters, who were wont to frequent the vicinity at this time, none was more remarkable
than old Sergeant Andrew Wallace.   He was a frequent

visitor at the Paoli and after Jones came in possession of the Green Tree, made this Inn his chief stopping place. Wallace was a veteran of the Revolution, and at that time (1833) was in the one hundred and fourth year of his age. He was married and had two children living, the youngest of which was then fourteen years old. The old sergeant had been a member of Captain Church's Company, in the Fourth Pennsylvania Regiment, commanded by Colonel Anthony Wayne, and participated in the battle of Brandywine, when Lafayette was wounded in that engagement. It was Sergeant Wallace, who rescued him from his perilous situation, and carried him off the field on his back for a distance of two miles to the house of a friend, where the illustrious Frenchman rested in safety.

The history of this remarkable man reads almost like a romance. Born in Scotland, March 14, 1730, he arrived in this country in 1752, after having participated, young as he was in the Batle of Culloden, on the side of the Stewarts. Shortly after his arrival in this country he enlisted at the breaking out of the French and Indian war in Captain Hannum's Company, at Chester. He was appointed at first as Orderly Sergeant. The company became part of the regular force under Colonel Dark, of Virginia, in General Forbes' division of Braddock's Army, but at the defeat of the latter his division was not in action.

At the very commencement of the Revolution Wallace enlisted, as above stated, in Wayne's Battalion, was again appointed to his former position as Sergeant, and served in that position until the end of the war. He was present at "Three Rivers," at Brandywine, and the affair at Paoli, where he had a narrow escape, and in after years he would never tire in relating how, when all was lost, that he jumped into a cluster of chestnut sprouts right in the midst of the British and Hessians and remained there in safety until the danger was over. The adventure did not deter him from at once reporting to his officer the next morning, and at the Battle of Germantown we find him in the midst of the affray. He passed through the encampment at Valley Forge, and the battle of Monmouth; but a few days later, while out on a scout, was taken prisoner together with Captain Sealery and eighteen comrades. Fortunately for him he was soon exchanged and he rejoined his command in time to volunteer and lead one wing of the "forlorn hope" in the storming of Stony Point. Afterwards he marched to South Carolina with his command and was present at the battles of Cowpens, Eutaw and Camden; also at the closing scene at Yorktown.

In 1785, he again enlisted at New Brunswick, New Jersey, under Captain Lane, to join Col. Harmer against the Mohawks. The troops, however, were discharged without seeing any service. A year later he again enlisted in the regular army and served on the Western frontier for three years. In the year 1791, he enlisted in Captain Doyle's company at Philadelphia, which was destined to form part of the ill fated command of General St. Clair against the Indians in the Western country. He was present at the dreadful slaughter which afterwards took place, and was one of the few who escaped the fury of the savages, and wounded and crippled as he was he made his way back to civilization to tell the tale of the disaster. In the affray he was shot in the arm, from the effects of which he never entirely recovered. This, however, did not deter him from remaining in the army, and in 1794 we find him once more under his old commander, General Wayne, fighting the savages on the banks of the Miami.

After the subjugation of the savages he served five years

SERGEANT ANDREW WALLACE.

AGED 104 YEARS (1833)

THE LAST SURVIVOR OF THE PAOLI MASSACRE.

in the United States Legion under Captain Pike. When this organization dissolved he went into Captain Schuyler's Company, Second Regiment, U. S. A. and marched with his regiment to New Orleans in 1812, and was finally discharged from the service in 1813 at the age of eighty years by General Wade Hampton, on account of debility, after almost 60 years of continuous service against the enemies of his adopted country. And now in his old age, after living long beyond the alloted period of life, we find the old veteran going from tavern to tavern selling pictures of himself to help eke out an existence for himself, wife and children. It is true he received a pension of twenty-six cents per day from the Government. How far that went to support the old veteran, palsy stricken and crippled as he was, need not be told. Colonel Isaac Wayne, a son of the General, together with other residents, however, saw that he did not want. The old man was always throughout his whole life temperate, steady, and regular; always avoiding excesses of any kind. By one of the identical pictures bought of him in person at the old inn, in 1833 and now before the writer, one would hardly think that the original was over seventy years of age, and was a veteran of the Revolution. His countenance even at his great age had a benign and intelligent expression, and although as before stated his body was continually shaken up with the palsy, and his right arm was somewhat crooked and stiff, he was in full possession of his mental faculties, with his mind and memory bright and clear. He was then the last survivor of all who were in the affair at Paoli. And on more than one occasion a party was made up at the inn to visit the battlefield in company with the old veteran, when he with pride would point out to one of the chestnut oak sprouts, which still remained but then grown to a clump of trees of considerable girth and size. He would also point out to the curious or inquisitive visitor the spot where his brother was killed by the cruel foe on that memorable night. Wallace died, January 27, 1835.

Politically the Green Tree became a rallying point for the Whigs, and became known as a "Whig House," and in consequence became the gathering place for many of that party, who heretofore had patronized the Paoli, the latter house under General Joshua Evans being the great rallying point for the Democracy. The polls of five townships, comprising what was then known as the "Paoli District" were held there. After the advent of Jonathan Jones at the Green Tree a determined effort was made to break up the Democratic stronghold at the Paoli. Ritner was elected Governor and the Anti-Masonic craze had about run its course, and the dismemberment of the district, commenced in 1823 by the separation of Charlestown township into an independent election district, was followed in 1838 by cutting off East Whiteland township, which now became the 32d district, with the polls at the General Wayne Inn, on the turnpike, near the 22d milestone. Willistown was constitüted the 35th district in 1839, with the polling place at the house of John Kimes, Sugartown. Easttown followed in 1840, and became the 39th district, with the voting place at the "Leopard," and to complete the matter three years later the polls at Tredyffrin were moved to New Centreville, in the Great Valley. Thus ended the political prestige of the Paoli.

For the next few years nothing of special importance took place until the year 1840. In the eight years since Jones came into possession of the old hostelry, the wooden sills on the railroad had been replaced by iron rails resting

THE WAYSIDE INNS ON THE LANCASTER ROAD.

CAMP WAYNE.

ON THE PAOLI BATTLE GROUND. 1877.

on wooden sleepers, the south track completed and steam motive power introduced. These improvements, however, were not an immediate success, and for a time the tracks were used both for steam and horse cars, an arrangement which led to endless contention between the rival interests. An account of some of the troubles of this early steam transportation will be given in a subsequent sketch. Eventually steam won the victory, when horse power was finally abolished. The travel on the turnpike also rapidly declined. Still, as before stated, the Tree was compensated by the patronage received from the new highway. About this time (1836), Jonathan Jones was succeeded by his son Jacob H. Jones, who proved as popular as his father had been with the patrons of the house. This state of affairs lasted until Wednesday, March 4, 1840, when the house was discovered to be on fire, it having caught from a spark from a passing locomotive, wood then being used exclusively as fuel and there being no provision for catching the flying sparks. The fire commenced on the roof, and although discovered in its earliest stage and the alarm promptly given, the fire was so rapid that before a ladder could be procured and mounted the fire was beyond extinguishment. In a short time there was nothing left standing but the blackened walls and smouldering ruins of the old hostelry. It was with great difficulty that the large barn and stables were saved from destruction, as the strong wind prevalent at the time carried the flames immediately towards them. The loss was estimated to be over $5000, there being no insurance. Considerable furniture was removed to a place of safety, but much of it in a greatly injured condition. In connection with this matter a curious anecdote was long prevalent in the neighborhood, viz: That among the willing helpers at the time there was none more active than a couple of the regular habitues of the barroom. At the first alarm these two men rushed upstairs and carefully carried down several feather beds, then returning threw the looking glasses and crockery out of the windows.

It was a curious coincidence that within that week three large fires occurred from sparks from locomotives, it was charged, through carelessness on the part of the engineers. The first of these was the large tavern barn at the Paoli, which then stood about where the present signal tower on the railroad stands, the dwelling house at the southwest corner of the overhead bridge then being the wagon shed. This happened February 26, 1840. This was followed by the destruction of the large tavern at Oakland, and finally, on March 4, our old landmark, the "Green Tree," in Willistown, was reduced to ashes. Fires along the line of the railroad, caused by sparks from the locomotives, became of such frequent occurrence that some of the county papers, opposed to the State Administration, boldly charged that a tavern or barn was set on fire on purpose every night so as to light the road.

The destruction of the old Inn after half a century of usefulness proved a serious loss to the owner; preparations were at once made to rebuild the Inn. It was decided, as the walls were so solid as to have withstood the devouring element, to add an additional story, making it a three story building. A temporary barroom was opened in an out-building, which had escaped the fire. This was used until the new house was completed. It became apparent early in the Summer that the annual parade and encampment of the military at the Paoli battle ground (not a mile from the Green Tree) would surpass anything of a similar character in previous years, consequently all efforts were strained to have the inn ready for business early in September. The Green Tree being the nearest public house to the grounds, was naturally well patronized on these occasions by both military and citizens, notwithstanding the fact that whiskey could be had at every farm house around the camp grounds. The affair, in 1840, was to last three days, and companies were expected from Philadelphia as well as from the adjoining counties.

The management of the affairs was entrusted mainly to Gen. Edward F. Evans, a brother of the Hon. Joshua Evans, of the Paoli. The projected encampment proved a great success, both as to the numbers and character of the participants, military and civil who were present on the occasion, prominent among whom were Governor David Rittenhouse Porter. The landlord of the Green Tree was not disappointed in his expectations of a rich harvest from the visitors to the camp.

After this spurt of business the new house settled down to the regular routine, with nothing but the weekly cattle sales and an occasional general vendue to break the monotony. A few years later, Jacob Jones left the house and went to Philadelphia, where he maintained his reputation as an inn keeper, presiding respectively over the West Chester House, on Broad street, the Indian Queen, on Fourth street, and the Rubicam House, on Sixth street. It was at the latter place that P. T. Barnum boarded Tom Thumb and other " freaks " on his first visit to the city. During this time the Green Tree was kept by Jonathan and Frank Jones. Jacob returned from the city about 1851, and again became the landlord, but shortly afterwards died.

Frank Jones for a time then presided over the fortunes of the old inn. He was preceded by Samuel Moore as tenant of the old tavern stand.

March 28, 1867, Jonathan Jones sold the property to John Crumley, during whose ownership Lewis J. Thomson and James Beale are said to have kept the bar. The passage of the "Local Option Law" in 1873, however, closed the bar for two years. In 1874 Crumley sold the property, Ex-Sheriff Gill being the purchaser. At the expiration of the Local Option law the house was relicensed. This, however, proved a matter of short duration. When the Pennsylvania Railroad straightened its road-bed in 1877-8 the new centre line was run directly through the house, necessitating its removal. The building was shortly afterwards demolished and there remains no vestige to remind the thousands of travelers who daily pass over the spot of its former existence.

Before closing this sketch it will not be amiss to state that for a number of years the Green Tree served as the Paoli Post Office. As before stated the Paoli under the regime of the Evans was a great Democratic stronghold. When in 1861 the great uprising of the populace took place, the post office was at once removed from the Paoli to the Green Tree. After the assassination of President Lincoln, during Johnson's term, the office was moved back to the Paoli; after General Grant's inauguration the office was at once returned to the "Green Tree." In 1880 application was made to the proper officials for the return of the office to Paoli, as the place had been sold to an "Improvement Company," and the increasing population needed better postal facilities. This was of course opposed by the residents in the vicinity of the "Tree," so after considerable discussion the citizens of the latter place consented to change the name of the office to "Duffryn Mawr." A new post office was then established at Paoli station under the time honored name of "Paoli."

THE "SHIP," IN WEST WHITELAND,

As Recollected by a Member of the "Old Hickory Club."

THE SHIP INN.

ON the afternoon of a bright spring day in April twenty-five years ago an enthusiastic amateur photographer, with outfit box in hand and tripod under his arm, trudged steadily up the turnpike, in West Whiteland, from Glen Loch towards Downingtown, stopped at Ship Lane to look at the neat chapel erected there. His eyes naturally wandered to the opposite corner, and being of a retrospective turn of mind he was mentally contrasting the present with the past, wondering whether the host of the old house, when in the height of its popularity, could ever have thought that the revolution of time in a few years would work changes so great as to leave the then magnifi-

cent and busy highway deserted and abandoned, and the
large number of inns by the roadside, houses large, roomy,
lofty, as they were, the owners trying to make each more at-
tractive to the travelling public than his competitors, and all
being hives of activity, now, after the lapse of a few years,
should no longer be houses of entertainment for man and
beast, but fenced in from the road, some idle, some used
as summer boarding houses, a few as private residences, or
occupied by tenants to prevent the property from falling
into decay, while others have been torn down or so remodeled that the fact of their having ever been noted public
houses is not even known to the present generation. While
these thoughts were occupying the mind of the amateur
he mechanically set up his tripod, adjusted his camera and
prepared to make a negative of what was left of the
former "Ship Tavern." While his attention was thus
engaged he had been joined by an elderly man, who had
been attracted to the spot by the appearance of the pseudo
artist. In the meantime the cap had been drawn and
returned, the exposure made and the plates carefully returned to the holder, when the old man, who from all
appearances was well on the shady side of the allotted three
score and ten, addressed the stranger. "Taking pictures
stranger?" Then continuing, "Do you know that house
you just took was once on a time a tavern? Yes. Well
don't forget it was a 'tavern' not a 'wagon stand.' Know
what a wagon stand is? Well this was the 'Ship.' Stages
and travelers stopped here. Strangers and travelers used
to call the house after the old signboard; it swung from
a yoke on a tall pole and had a big ship painted on it; it
was a curious old sign, it used to swing and creak so when
the wind blew at nights some people used to get scared at
the noise it made. I often heard my grandfather say how,
long before the revolution the same old sign used to swing

in front of a tavern on the old Lancaster road beyond Downingtown, long before the pike was thought of. Well, this tavern-keeper was a Tory, and when after the Battle of Brandywine a lot of American soldiers came that way, and halting at the house, and not getting a very courteous reception from the old Tory, they got mad and before they left shot thirteen bullets through the signboard—for bad luck as they said to the crusty old Tory. Somehow, after that the old house didn't prosper any more like it formerly had, so after the pike was built and things got so busy along the smooth, hard road, this house was built and called the "Ship" and the old sign was brought down and set up anew, thirteen holes and all. All houses in that day had signboards with pictures on them. This was necessary, for many of the teamsters along the road could not read; others were Pennsylvania Dutchmen and couldn't understand English letters, but all knew the pictures and would know a house when they came to it. We, however, who lived around here, knew the old 'Ship' for years and years only as the 'Widow Evans'.' Queer—how was that? Well mistress Susie Evans kept that house for over forty years. The first I recollect of her was about 1820, when Major Bowen kept the house, and Susie was his wife. Well about ten years after that Bowen died, and it was not long before his widow married Levi Evans, and they carried on the house—we all used to know her then as Susie Evans—however Levi did not live long, and Susie was again left a widow. She still kept the house until she died just before the war broke out. That is how the house got to be known to everybody as the Widow Evans'. Well, after she died the old house ceased to be a tavern, and the property was sold to a French family from the city, who I hear lately sold it again. Many a night, continued the old resident, I spent in that barroom; there was plenty of whiskey about then, we didn't have to tramp all the way to Downingtown for it, and such as it is, why 'taint worth drinking after you do get it nowadays.   But as I was saying the whiskey, as well as the people, were different then. The widow Evans used to get her whiskey from a still over by the Springs, I mean the Yellow Springs, over the hill there, another lively place when I was a boy.   Colonel Bowen used to keep the house over there."

Along about sixty-five years ago Mr. Chambers, the celebrated divine and temperance lecturer, came up from Philadelphia to deliver a lecture on temperance at Grove, in Chester County.   He left the train at Oakland Station, now Whitford, and before going across he entered the hotel at that place and requested Mr. Boyer to give him "a strong cup of coffee."   A Mrs. Evans, who kept the Ship tavern, in the same township, heard of the incident, and in presence of some parties she made use of the expression that she wished he had come to her with that request: "I would have made it strong enough for him."

This expression of Mrs. Evans reached the ears of Mr. Chambers and a few days later in a lecture down at Everhart's grove in West Chester he made allusion to the matter in terms not at all complimentary to Mrs. Evans. It so happened that that lady had a goodly number of friends in the audience and they took exceptions to his remarks and were disposed to make things unpleasant for him.

A correspondent expresses himself on the condition of things temperate at that period:

"You might have thought by the efforts the temperance people were making in those days liquor would have been wiped from the face of the earth before this.   They did succeed in wiping it out of the township of West Whiteland so far as licensed hotels were concerned.   In speaking of Mrs. Evans and the Ship, there was no place where temperance people would rather go for a good meal than at the Ship, for they were sure to get a good, strong cup of coffee and plenty of brandy in their mince pie."

Like everybody else, those good old temperance people liked good living, and went where it was to be had.

"There were no temperance folks around here then— things were different. No matter how much of the widow's whiskey I drank, it never gave me a headache the next day—but it is different now—the liquor has changed and so has the times around here. You see that big house yonder on the right. Well, that is Jacob's; and there is a large ore-bank and quarry which was worked then, and many a load of ore and stone was hauled out of it, to say nothing of the many men who were employed there. Then after a time they struck several big springs, so they put in steam pumps, banked up a field and formed a small lake of about twenty acres. You can see it right below the house, what is left of it looks like a big earthwork or fort, like we built on the Arlington Heights in '61 to save Washington. Then you see that house just below the old dam? That is the old 'Sheaf of Wheat,' or 'Wheat Sheaf,' that was a wagon stand, not a stage tavern—like the 'Ship.' But, stranger, the greatest time I remember around here was the year I first voted. Andy Jackson was my man, and we re-elected him. Old Hickory we called him, and our club was the 'Old Hickory Club' and we met at the 'Ship.' There were good times around here then. There was plenty of good whiskey around here when we met, and none of your patent stuff like nowadays neither. I lived just below the line in East Whiteland and had to go all the way to General Evans' (Paoli) to get my vote in. However, there was plenty of fun that election, there was no end to it. Almost everybody except we of the 'Old

Hickory' creed was an 'Anti.'   Don't know what I mean
by an Anti—well, I might have known that you wouldn't
know.   It came about this way.   There were a lot of men,
or a society, that used to meet around at different taverns
in West Chester, Downingtown, at the 'Jackson,' below
Paoli, at 'Filson's,' up in Humphrysville, and at the 'Olive
Branch,' on the Harrisburg pike.   These clubs or meetings were called Freemasons, and the members were most
all well-to-do citizens.   Well, some men who wanted to
join them and couldn't, because they were not wanted, got
mad and called the members 'Cabletows,' and even accused
them of murdering people.   Well, stranger, as these
Masons took no notice of these things, it only made the
outsiders madder, and they formed a political party and
started two papers in the county, one at West Chester by
Joseph Painter, the other at Coatesville by Dr. Perkins.
This party called themselves the 'Anti's,' and it was not
long before they made things hot in the county, and in
almost no time every man around here excepting us was an
'Anti' of some kind.   There was—let me see— the 'anti-
Jacksons,' 'anti-Masons,' 'anti-Republicans,' 'anti-Whigs,'
'anti-Canals,' 'anti-Taxations' and others, but no matter
how strong an 'anti' they were, or how excited or worked
up they would get, on one point they all agreed with the
'Old Hickory Club.'   What was that?   Why that come
what may there should be no 'anti-whiskey.'   But Mister,
as I was saying, there was a great election.   There was no
end to the fun, even the Lancaster county Dutchmen teaming along the pike got warmed up, and when they would
pass a Jackson house or see anybody out on the porch they
would sing

> " ' Wart nur dee Irisher
> der Josef Ritner is der mon
> der unser Staat regiren Kon.'

" Ritner was their candidate for Governor, he was the
' Boss-Anti.' Our man was George Wolfe.

" After harvest was over the weather and politics kept
on getting hotter and hotter—so did the Anti's, and they
kept threatening things, so in August our County Committee met at Gallagherville, up above Downington, and
formed Vigilance Committees for every township in the
county. Two of our club were named for West Whiteland, Enos Strickland and John T. Worthington. Never
heard of them. Well, Mister, I recollect them just as if
it was last week. The committee was no sooner appointed
than we got a scare around here that made a good many
forget all about politics for a time. What was that?
Why, Mister, it was a new disease to us, they called it
cholera. At first it didn't scare us; the club met right
along. We were not afraid, as everybody said that whiskey was a sure cure for the new disease, and any one
who drank plenty of it wouldn't take it. You suppose
a good many took the cure for fear of the cholera; you are
right, stranger. However, one day it broke out down by
Kunkle's mill, right over there in the Valley—know where
it is? Yes, well there were eleven taken in two days, and
nine died, for all the whiskey they drank it didn't help
them. We stopped our meeting for a while then, but after
a little, people got over their scare, and the disease left our
county, and it wasn't long before the fun started up again.
The Anti's blamed the whole thing upon the Cabletows,
or Freemasons. Some even blamed the whiskey, others
allowed it was all the fault of the Jackson men. The

'Hickory Club,' however, went right on, drank Susie Evans' whiskey, and stood up for Jackson, Wilkins and Wolfe. Well, stranger, that puts me in mind of when the weather got cooler in the fall. As the time for election came nearer, our Congressman, General Joshua Evans, got up a great rally at his tavern at Paoli. We had elected Wolfe at the October election, and the Anti's were pretty sick. I'll never forget that as long as I live. What day was it? Why the twenty-seventh of October, 1832. Mister, they don't have meetings like this one was any more. The General and his brother Edward engineered the whole thing that day. They called it the great rally of the 'Democracy against the Aristocracy.' Five townships used to vote at Paoli then, and you should have seen how the people flocked to the Paoli on that day. Every road and lane that led to the Paoli was alive with men and boys in stages, wagons, on horseback and on foot. You might a thought the whole county was on the go. But, Mister, you should have seen the 'Old Hickory Club' as they came down the pike, four abreast. Strickland and Worthington, our marshals, were ahead. Then came the buglers. Joseph Free was one of them, and he could bugle. He bugled for the 'Lafayette Rangers,'—they used to meet at the Ship too. What were the Rangers? Why I was one of them, they were a soldier company, and part of the 143rd Regiment Pennsylvania Militia. George Wagonseller used to drill and muster us up at the 'Ship'; but, as I was saying, after the buglers came a horseman with a brand new American flag, and that flag had twenty-six stars on it, remember that, Mister. Then we as had horses followed mounted, each rank made up according to the color of the horses. Then came a long string of hay wagons, dearborns, and the like filled with members who didn't have any horses. These wagons were all trimmed up with cedar and shellbark boughs, and how we all cheered for 'Old Hickory' as we went past the Sheaf, Steamboat, Wayne, Warren and the Tree. But, stranger, times like these have passed and gone long ago—you will never see a turnout like that was now—times is so changed. But Mister you should have heard the cheering when we come down the pike at Paoli. The General had old 'Diana' there, and they fired her off as soon as they saw our flag coming over the hill at Thomas' shops. Diana? Why that was a big brass cannon and belonged to the Paoli Artillerists. When we got down to the State road, you should have heard the band at the tavern yard play 'Independence Day has Come' and 'Yankee Doodle.' They don't play tunes like these nowadays, Mister." After a short pause, during which the old man seemed to be lost in thought, he continued. "There was plenty of whiskey there that day, not bottles either, but barrels with spiggots in them. 'Here is to Old Hickory,' and 'Down with the Aristocrats' were the toasts and many a one was drunk. The whiskey wasn't as good as we got at Susie's, but everybody drank as much as they could get of it anyhow. Stranger, they don't have meetings like this nowadays. Times ain't what they used to be. One thing about this rally, however, always struck me as queer when I think about it. What was that? Why there wasn't an Anti for miles around who was not there, and how they all pitched into the Jackson whiskey got me.

"When election day came around we beat them all and re-elected Old Hickory, but times have changed since then. Why stranger, many a time I stood right here on this spot and counted over fifty 'Pitt teams' in a string pass me both ways, one right after another. 'Pitt teams' were six-

horse teams. The wagons had extra broad tires on the
wheels, some were loaded as heavy as six tons weight, and
they teamed through to Pittsburgh beyond the mountains.
They don't make wagons like these now, but as I was saying times have changed. First they started to build the
railroad, but they were a long time getting it to work right.
Then things went from bad to worse. They got locomotives and trains on the railroad, the canal was finished
from Columbia to the mountains and one of the first things
they did was to put wheels under the canal boats and haul
them over the railroad between the inclined planes at
Columbia and Belmont on the Schuylkill. Why, stranger,
I have stood here on the pike many a time and seen the
trains of boats hauled past here—they were freight as well
as passenger boats—'packets' they called them. They
were built in sections, painted white, green shutters to the
windows outside and Turkey red curtains inside—seems
curious now. Not long after this, the traffic on the pike
went down, stages were taken off, teaming was done for,
tavern after tavern shut up, first the wagon stand, then one
stage house after another—and here we are to-day, the
pike full of ruts and holes, abandoned and deserted. The
widow Evans dead and gone long ago and the 'Ship,' well
stranger, if any one would have said anything like this
would ever happen when the 'Hickory Club' met there—
well, he would have been taken for a lunatic and put where
he could do no harm, but times have changed. After things
got so bad years ago I got disheartened and joined the
'Battleaxes'; then I got into more trouble and left this
part of the country until last year, when I came back to die.
Would I like to have a picture of the old inn? Well
stranger, replied the old man, you're a stranger to me and
very clever; I'm obliged to you for being so kind, but I

have got no use for it this way, but show me one of the 'Ships' as it was when the widow Evans kept it. The Hickory's met there and drank her whiskey, with the never-ending line of teams, stages and droves traveling by on the smooth white turnpike, with the old wheelwright shop and smithy at the opposite corner (it's a tenant house now), where I so often stopped when a boy to watch the men at work over the fire on the hearth, and listen to the sound of the hammer on the anvil. Let me see a picture with the old tree, pump and water trough, the crowds and loungers on the porch, and a stage—one of the 'Good Intent' or 'Opposition' lines, don't matter which—with their four dapple grays drawn up, prancing in the old yard. Show me a picture, stranger, like this. Put it up at vendue and I will bid until I get it. I hope," continued the old resident with a look of sadness on his face, " that I have not given you any offence with my talk, but I felt young again. When you come this way again go to Downingtown. There are two houses there you ought to take. Would I like to go along and tell you what I know about the houses on the pike from Paoli to Downing-town? Well, Mister, you are very kind to want an old man like me for company, but come up and I will tell you what I can remember. But one thing is sure; in all my travels I never came across any whiskey to come up to the widow Evans'. Good bye!" After this parting shot in praise of the former refreshment dispensed in the old inn, the old resident pattered slowly up the pike, while the amateur stood thinking about the picture of long ago which the old man had conjured up before him. The long shadows of the sun, however, soon awakened him from his reverie, and he at once saw that his day's work was done. So quickly had the minutes passed. Picking up his tripod and plate holders he sadly turned his back to the setting sun and trudged wearily over the deserted highway towards the station at Glen Loch, making at the same time the mental resolve in the near future to again seek out the old member of the " Hickory Club."

AFTER THE VENDUE.

THE WAYSIDE INNS ON THE LANCASTER ROAD.

THE "SIGN OF THE WHITE HORSE".

ON THE OLD LANCASTER ROAD IN EAST WHITELAND, CHESTER COUNTY, PENNSYLVANIA.

"THE SIGN OF THE WHITE HORSE" IN EAST WHITELAND.

THE WHITE HORSE.

IN East Whiteland township, in the very heart of the Great Valley, at the cross roads formed by the Swedeford and the road from Glenloch to the Yellow Springs, there is a pleasantly situated hamlet known as the White Horse. It consists, besides the usual general store, blacksmith and wheelright shops, of about half a dozen houses. To the usual visitor there is nothing to distinguish the village from dozens of similar ones in the county. There is one house, however, that has a history dating back to the earliest settlement of the Great Valley. This house is at the eastern end of the village, and is now used as an ordinary farm house. It can be easily recognized by the porch which opens to the road, extends along the whole front of the house, also by the two ends of the building being of different heights.

This small unpretentious structure was formerly one of the most famous inns in the State and known far and near as "The Sign of the White Horse." It was one of the first licensed houses in the county, and it was not long before the spot became one of the most active centers in the County of Chester, and as will be seen was an important stopping place in provincial, colonial and revolutionary times, even maintaining its prestige for a considerable time after the construction of the turnpike had diverted the bulk of the travel and patronage from the former "great road" from Philadelphia to Lancaster.

The eastern end of the old tavern with its low ceiling dates from the first half of the eighteenth century, while the western part was built towards the end of the century —tradition says after the close of the Revolution.

The walls originally were of rough stone, pointed, as all houses of that period were built, but of late they have been plastered over or dashed with a coating of yellow mortar, and now give the visitor of the present day but little idea of the former appearance of the house, nor is there anything about it now to show any sign of the former importance of the place as a landmark, or that it once was a haven of shelter and rest for the weary wayfarer and an asylum for all classes of the community from the devout missionary, on his way through the forest to supply his widely separated charges—to the hardy teamsters of the colonial period, who availed themselves of the good cheer dispensed within the narrow limits of its walls.

An old manuscript map of old Chester county, supposed from all indications to have been made prior to 1744, was found some years ago among a lot of old papers, and fortunately came to the hands of the writer; though unartistic and crude in execution and design, it cannot fail to prove a valuable document to the student of our early county history.

Prominent among the few landmarks by the roadside depicted on the map is the "White Horse" in Whiteland. At the time the map was made it was the fifth on the way from the Schuylkill to the Brandywine, viz.:—"The Buck," "Radnor Meeting," "The Ball," "Warren," then "The White Horse," on the banks of the Valley creek. The situation being a most important center, the King's highway, which replaced the old Indian path or trail, and known after 1733 as the Lancaster road, here branched off or forked; the right hand road leading to the Conestoga settlements by way of the "Red Lyon," while the left hand branch led to Downing's mill on the Brandywine.

The road from Chester, then known as the "Edgmont" road, terminated and intersected with the Lancaster road near this point.

Another road known as the "Moore Hall" road led from this common center to the Schuylkill fords and points beyond that stream as well as towards Vincent and Valley Forge.

The main road of the Chester Valley known to this day as the Swedeford road also converged into the Lancaster road a short distance east of the White Horse. This road was ordered by the Provincial Council held May 6, 1724, "as the most convenient for the publick, and especially necessary for the congregation of Baptists and of least detriment to private persons."

As will be seen the centering of these various roads tended at even this early day to give this point an advantage over almost any other tavern stand in the county, and it was destined to become one of the busiest centers between Philadelphia and what is now known as Downingtown.

The exact year when the first house was built or when

the first license was granted is difficult to determine. It is known, however, to have been very early in the century.

When James Thomas, a Welshman, erected his primitive log structure in the almost unbroken wilderness, it might be said to have been on the very outskirts of civilization.

The only means of communication with the older settlements was the well trodden Indian path or trail, which led from the Schuylkill to the Brandywine. Indians were still numerous in the vicinity, and as a general thing friendly to the whites; there was no scarcity of game, and the settler only feared the wild beasts which abounded in the Valley hills.

James Thomas served as constable of the township as early as 1711, and as strong liquors were thought to be the best antidote against any or all diseases indigenous to the new country, they soon became indispensable to the settler and were in universal use by all classes of the community. The tradition that Thomas kept an inn at the time he served as constable, or shortly afterward, is further strengthened by the fact that, in 1715, he is assessed double the amount of any other resident of the township. The first official record relating to the house, which is still in existence, is the application of James Thomas for license in 1721, when he applied for a license to keep a "house of entertainment, for selling wine, brandy, rum and other strong liquors."

The few appointments and furniture of this rude cabin in the forest were no doubt all of the most simple character and it seems to us of the present day as if the house itself had been established far in advance of those who were to form the inn-keeper's future support.

In the next year, 1722, Thomas was succeeded by

Edward Kennison, who, strange to say, had also been Thomas's successor as constable in 1712. Under Kennison's ownership the house seems to have flourished and at once became a local landmark.

As the travel increased the old Indian trail through the forest became a bridle or "packer" path; and for some years following the opening of the house, all liquors and necessaries required at the inn were brought on pack horses from Philadelphia or Chester. Shortly after Kennison's advent an effort was made by the citizens of Chester county to have the "King's Highway" and public road from Philadelphia to Conestoga, through Merion and Radnor, put in passable condition for cart or wagon travel as far as the Brandywine; this effort followed by a petition from the citizens of Lancaster in 1731 and others of similar import from Chester county in 1735, eventually resulted in the opening, in 1741, of what became known as the "Great" or Lancaster road.

In 1735 another petition was presented to the Provincial Council "of sundry inhabitants of the county of Chester and Lancaster setting forth the Want of a High Road in the remote parts of the Counties, and that a very commodious one may be laid out from the ferry of John Harris on the Susquehannah to fall in with the high Road from Lancaster Town, at or near the Plantation of Edward Kennison, in the Great Valley of Chester County, &c., &c." This was also granted and formed another artery of travel leading from this common center.

When the primitive log cabin was enlarged by the erection of the eastern part of the present structure is not definitely known, but it was no doubt built at the time when these roads were opened, about 1735–40.

A well founded and plausible tradition tells us that this

log house stood where the western end now stands, and when the needs of traffic demanded it the eastern end was built, and when after the Revolution this house in turn proved inadequate to the demands upon it, the log part in turn gave way to the present west or new end.

Another curious thing about this house was the precaution which was taken to resist any attack upon the inmates by the Indians in case of an uprising, which was so much dreaded about the middle of the eighteenth century. To prevent being cut off from water, a wooden pipe or trunk was laid from the hill back of the house conveying the water from a spring in the hillside through the cellar to a shallow well in front of the house, a pump in which supplied the uses of travelers and teamsters; in case of necessity a plug could be withdrawn in the cellar and thus give an ample supply of water to the inmates without leaving the sheltering walls of the house. These tubes or pipes remained in the place until removed by the present owner a little over three decades ago, when the house was put in its present condition.

An old account of the inn describes the table as being of split slabs, supported by round legs set in auger holes, the stools three-legged, and made in the same manner; wooden pins, stuck in the walls at the back, supported some clapboards which served for shelves for the table furniture. This consisted of pewter dishes, plates, and spoons, but mostly of wooden bowls, trenchers, and noggins; if the last run short, gourds or hard shell squashes made up the deficiency.

As to the bill of fare, for breakfast it was usually coffee, hog and hominy, while potpie was the main standby for dinner; for supper tea and coffee with mush and milk was the usual fare. During the fall and winter, however, there was no lack of venison and game, the neighboring Valley hills furnishing an abundance of those luxuries, while in summer the product of the truck patch, such as greens (beet tops), corn, pumpkins, beans and potatoes added variety to the almost monotonous menu.

Pegs around the walls answered for the great coats or hats of such guests who were too dainty to place their clothing on the sanded floor as was done by the majority of travelers.

In the tap room most of the liquor was dispensed from stone jugs, pewter mugs being used exclusively for drinking purposes. The liquor was always measured out to the patron. When more was wanted a second drink was charged. In 1741 the price of a drink of rum was three pence.

At this time there were still many Indians in the vicinity especially towards Pequea and the Brandywine. As the settlers increased in numbers more or less trouble arose between the Indians and the newcomers, as the game which was the sustenance of the aborigines decreased and became scarce, the Indians were apt to prey on their white neighbors. This gave cause for numerous complaints. One claim was filed as late as October 3, 1727, when sundry Indians killed a cow belonging to Richard Thomas who lived near our old inn.

While in the same year the Indians complained to the council of the encroachments of the whites and the obstructions in the Brandywine when the Sheriff was directed to "throw the same down." The Indians continued in the valley until about 1755, when the French and Indian War broke out, when they generally removed beyond the bounds of the county.

We have no records relating to the hostelry until at the

commencement of the Indian troubles, when the inn seems to have been kept by one John Neely, who is said to have been there prior to 1753. From an entry in Rodger Hunt's account book June 10, 1759, we find: "To expenses at the White Horse, John Neely's, 3s, 6d." It also is mentioned on the several military documents of the time, the distance given thereon from the Court House at Philadelphia, is 26 miles, 1 quarter, 18 perches.

Presumably Neely kept the house until 1762, when Thomas Lemans or Lemmons was at the White Horse. His name does not again appear. His successor for the next year was probably Owen Ashton.

Then John Kerlin appears on the records as host. Little is known of him until the year 1774, when he, together with Anthony Wayne, Francis Johnson, Sketchly Morton and other citizens of the county were elected a committee at Chester, December 20th, "to carry into execution the association of the late Continental Congress, and to be and continue from this time until one month after the rising of the next Continental Congress, &c., &c." From the above it may be gleaned that Kerlin was an influential member of the community, as well as a patriot.

When scarcely three years later, the ruthless invader, with his Hessian hirelings, overran with heavy tread our peaceful and fertile valley in his attempt to capture the city, Kerlin, in common with his patriotically inclined neighbors, suffered severe loss during the short occupation of the terrain by the British, everything that was of use or could be caried off was taken, while the remainder was burned or destroyed, it is said, in a fire made in front of the house, with the bean poles, paling and rails from the adjoining garden.

The original claim for this loss, filed by John Kerlin, is now in possession of the Pennsylvania Historical Society, viz.:

"An amount of the Damages John Kerlin received by the army under the Command of General How in his march from Brandywine to Philadelphia, Sept. 18th, 1777."

Among the losses mentioned are:

"To table linnin—towels, &c............£ 10—0—0
Wairing apparel both womans and mens.... 10—0—0
To Chainy bowls—plates and tea ware, &c. 35—0—0
To Earthen ware and bottles........... 3—0—0
The total amount summed up to   £199—0—0 "

The account was affirmed to before Benjamin Bartholomew November, 1782.

From the fact that this claim does not mention any liquors having been seized or destroyed it is probable that his stock was removed to a place of safety before the British army reached the valley.

It was on the high ground or plateau south of this house where General Washington determined, September 16, 1777, to risk another battle with the British, with the view of saving the city of Philadelphia. It is said that the selection of the ground was Washington's own choice. There was considerable skirmishing between the advance forces of the two armies and a sanguinary battle would no doubt have resulted, but a sudden thunderstorm of great violence stopped its progress.

Had the fates permitted this battle to continue it is probable that it would have been a decisive action which would have had most serious consequences. Had the British army, under Howe and Cornwallis, suffered on that day a signal defeat it would then and there have assured

American independence, while on the contrary if it had ended in the decided defeat or overthrow of Washington, we might at the present time still be living under the rule of the Lion and the Unicorn, with no use for fireworks on the fourth of July.

When three months later the American army went into winter quarters at Valley Forge, almost within sight of our hamlet, the point was of great importance to Washington.   The inn was selected as the first stopping place and relay station for the express riders between headquarters and Lancaster where Congress was then holding its sessions.   One of the most trusted of these messengers was the son of Captain Patrick Anderson, of the Line, and whose peaceful home was but a few miles northeast of the old inn.

After the tide of war had receded from the fertile valley, the recuperation of the residents was necessarily slow, still by thrift and industry the damages were gradually repaired—fences were replaced, damaged buildings repaired and cattle were again seen browsing in the meadows.   The travel on the Lancaster road increased until it became the great highway to the West, the old inn reaped its share of patronage and Kerlin soon recovered from his losses. Shortly after peace was assured, a successful attempt was made to run a stage coach on the road between Philadelphia and Lancaster, but this was done only after repeated failures.

This line to Lancaster was established in April, 1785, by Frederick Doersh and William Weaver, who state that their "Stage Wagon" will set out every Monday and Friday mornings from the King of Prussia Tavern, in Market street above third; and from the Black Horse Tavern, Queen street, Lancaster, every Tuesday and

Saturday mornings. Each passenger was allowed fourteen pounds of baggage. The fare was twenty shillings,
one half to be paid on entering the name in the book.

For some reason the proprietors of the stage did not
get along harmoniously, and in the latter part of the next
year (1786) the following card was displayed in the barroom of the inn, which was from the start a main stopping
place of the "Stage Wagon."

"Stage Coach,"

The partnership of Weaver and Doersh, late proprietors of the
stage from Lancaster to Philadelphia, is this day dissolved by
mutual consent.

The stage coach, with the mail, in future will be carried only
by the subscribers who have provided themselves with a sufficient
and easy coach upon a much better and easier construction than
any hitherto used, together with a set of excellent and strong
horses and a well experienced and careful driver, and will pay the
strictest attention in the receiving and delivering of subscribers,
articles, letters and packets. The stage coach with the mail will
set out from the House of the subscriber, Adam Weaver, at the
sign of the Black Horse in Lancaster, every Monday morning
precisely at 6 o'clock, and arrive at Philadelphia every Tuesday at
the House of John Stein, in Market street, at the sign of the
Black Bear. And will start for Lancaster from the sign of the
Black Bear every Thursday at 6 o'clock precisely, and arrive at
the House of Adam Weaver every Friday.

The proprietors flatter themselves by their former conduct and
unwearied attention, to those who were pleased to favor them with
their custom that they will afford general satisfaction as the entertainment at the House in Lancaster is well known, and particularly the attention paid to travelers, in Philadelphia, at Mr. Stein's,

will render the entertainment agreeable and worthy the notice of gentlemen and ladies traveling in the stage, by

The public's most humble servants,

WEAVER & PFLIEGER.

December 23d, 1786.

But this, like the other similar enterprise, was soon abandoned, caused mainly by the bad condition of the road, and the uncertainty of arriving at the place of destination at the advertised time.   A clergyman who, in 1786, attempted the journey thus describes his experience on reaching the White Horse: "The horses could only walk most of the way, the stage wagon was in frequently to the axletree, and I had no sooner recovered from a terrible plunge on one side than there came another in the opposite direction, and confounded all my efforts to preserve a steady sitting.   I was the only passenger, and it took the four horses, with the empty wagon seven hours to go the twenty-three miles."

At this time the tavern was much frequented, as well as the gathering place of farmers for miles around, and, except on market days, the barroom and porch would usually be filled with drovers, teamsters and men from the country, whips or sticks in hand, swinging on chairs or lounging at the bar, driving their bargains; in fact it was a sort of an agricultural exchange.

If the day and road were fair a number could always be seen playing "Long Bullets," the favorite pastime of the day.   The game consisted in seeing who could roll iron cannon balls, relics of the Revolution, the greatest distance along the road, similar to the present ten pin ball.   The one who rolled the shortest ball having to gather up and bring all the balls to the base.

The White Horse was also a favorite stopping place for bands of Indians, who at that time (1790–1800) would make frequent visits to the capital city, bringing down skins and furs, which they would barter for lead, stockings, pipes, etc., etc.

On arriving at the inn they would always ask for rum and sugar of which they were very fond; if refused, they would offer to shoot pennies for it; this was done by fixing a copper cent on a stick and set up from 30 to 50 yards from the dusky marksman, who would then shoot at it with his bow and arrow. If he hit the cent, which he usually did, the coin belonged to him, if not he tried it over again, this afforded much amusement to strangers and children, beside slacking the savage's thirst. When stopping over night they would sleep in the barn or, if cold, on the kitchen floor.

The house at this period was also a favorite stopping place with the German farmers on their way to and from the city with their loads of grain or provisions. Economy with these people was the order of the day, money was sparingly spent, and traveling expenses were reduced to a minimum. Most of these farmers carried their own food, even their necessary whiskey was brought from home. In the winter they formed a curious scene at night as they lay stretched out on the floor in a wide circle around the barroom stove, with feet towards the fire, each man on his own straw sack and covered with his coat or quilt, sleeping the sleep of the weary, only to be on the road again long before the first streak of dawn. In connection with these people it was a curious fact that the innkeeper could always tell how the markets were by the crack of their whips as they approached the tavern; if good their whips would crack incessantly, if the contrary the whip was in the socket.

With the advent of the year 1787 came a new landlord, Arthur Rice, who deserves more than a passing notice. Rice had been a volunteer scout during the Revolution, and was one of Washington's most trusted scouts. It is said that during the encampment of Valley Forge, Rice who was a man of powerful physique, on one occasion captured single handed two British or Hessian soldiers and brought them together with their arms and accoutrements, within the American lines. For this act of bravery and daring he was complimented by the Commander-in-Chief. He afterwards rendered valuable services to the army, notably at the battle of Monmouth, for all of which he would never receive a penny of pay or reward. He was also a Past Master of the Masonic Fraternity, which met in the Valley during the encampment.

So great did Washington value the services Rice had rendered and his disinterestedness and patriotism, that while President he would invariably send invitations to festal occasions and levee to the humble inn keeper at the "Sign of the White Horse."

The house now became a regular meeting place for the ex-soldiers who resided in the Valley and who had formerly been members of some of the Military Lodges in the Revolution Army, or of the Historic Lodge No. 8, which met at Valley Forge. These meetings soon resulted in an application to the Grand Lodge of Pennsylvania for a warrant to hold a lodge in the Chester Valley. This petition was granted and it was in the second-story room of the eastern end of the old inn, on the sixth day of December, 1790, that the altar of Free Masonry was re-erected in the Great Valley and Lodge 50 constituted. Who the members were and the history of the Lodge, how it afterwards became the most influential one in the country until it succumbed to public opinion during the Anti-Masonic crusade, has been fully told previously by the writer. The furniture of the Lodge room consisted of plain hickory chairs and settees. The Master's chair is still in the possession of a descendant of Arthur Rice. Two engravings or charts hung against the wall, these were preserved for many years, but at present unfortunately cannot be found. After the Lodge got fairly under way, on several occasions, entertainments and balls were given, which were great social events, and attracted all the youth and beauty in the vicinity for miles around. From 1791 to 1793, for some reason James Bones, a brother-in-law of Arthur Rice, appeared as inn keeper. The following year Rice again was in charge and remained so until his death in 1796. He was succeeded by his widow Jane Rice in 1797, who kept the Inn until her marriage to Stephen Bowen, who was also a prominent member of the Masonic Lodge that met at the Inn. Bowen appeared in charge until his death in 1810, when the goods and chattels were appraised and sold. Bowen was also a prominent member of H. R. A. Chapter, No. 75, and his Masonic marks and jewels are still treasured by his descendants.

It was during the terms of Rice and Bones that the turnpike was constructed at this point a mile to the south, and the great bulk of travel diverted.

After the sale by Bowen's widow the house came into possession of John Pearce, a brother to Colonel Cromwell Pearce, who kept it until after 1817, when it came into the possession of Samuel Ritenbaugh in whose possession and later that of his sons it remained for many years, becoming, however, known more as a drove stand.

One of the curious sights, common in the fall of the year, half a century ago, were flocks or droves of fowls, generally turkeys, but now and then also geese, being driven towards the city. The task of driving a turkey army, as such a flock or drove was called, was not an easy one by any means. The great danger was that they were apt to crowd together and trample each other to death; to prevent this they were divided into different lots, and a boy or man, called a "shooer," placed in charge of each section. Each driver, or shooer, armed with a long pole or rod, with a piece of red flannel fastened to the end had charge of about from fifty to seventy fowls; the best time made on the road by an army of this kind, while on the march, was not much over one mile an hour, even this speed, however, decreased towards nightfall, for as soon as it commenced to grow dark the birds were determined to go to roost, and then the fun commenced, and notwithstanding all the efforts of the drivers to the contrary the turkeys generally gained their point. This stampede usually took place in passing an orchard or copse of trees, when in much less time than it takes to relate it, the trees were black with birds, and the day's journey ended for the turkeys. Not so for the drivers, whose duty it was to watch the fowls and prevent them from getting "mixed up" with any other turkeys in the neighborhood, or being raided by evilly disposed persons. For this purpose the drivers always had a covered wagon, in which some of the men slept while the others remained on guard. On account of the slow progress of the fowls the droves always kept away from the much traveled turnpike and confined their route to the less frequented highways.

It was Ritenbaugh who replaced the old provincial log barn with the fine stone structure which now stands by the roadside. The old smithy that for years stood near the old inn was also removed to its present location at the cross roads. Toward the latter years of Ritenbaugh's ownership he voluntarily gave up the tavern, refusing to take out a license. From that time the place ceased to be a tavern stand, after an existence as such for almost a century and a half. Soon afterwards the place was sold and came into the possession of one of Philadelphia's well known capitalists, by whom it was remodeled and repaired, and now, as stated at the beginning of this sketch, does duty as a quiet farm house.

INDEX.

A

Admiral Vernon, The, 45
Admiral Warren, The, 45
Aston, George, 48, 49
André, Major, 52, 53, 54
Anti-Masonry, 178

B

Black Horse, 17, 25
Buck Tavern, 17
Black Bear, 19, 95; Sketch of, 102;
John Philips, 103; revolutionary
history, *ib.*
Blue-Ball, 11, 19, 95; Old Prissy
Robinson, 100; Portrait, 101;
Gruesome Tales of the, 48–51
Blue-Ball (Halfway house), 80;
petition for license, 82; for road,
83; Peter Kalm, *ib.;* name
changed to King of Prussia, 85;
Headquarters for General Forbes,
85; Bernhardus Van Leer, 86;
a trip for pleasure, 87; bad
roads, 88; legal prices for
liquors, 89–90; highway robbers,
90; Fitz and Dougherty, *ib.;*
Christopher Marshall, 91; difficulties of travel, 92; pastimes, 93
Barley Sheaf, 24
" Baer's," 25

C

Conestoga Wagons, 12, 37
Columbus Tavern, 16
Cross-keys, 23, 25
Clemson's Tavern, 26
Conestoga Inn, 27

Clemson, James, 31
Clingers, 36, 96
Coachees, 38
Columbia Railway, 116, 163; First
Accident on, 163
Coffman, Henry, 161
Chambers, Rev. John, 176

D

Drove Stands, 7
Distance Tables, 8, 11
Durham Ox, 16
" Downings," 61, 62; Post Office, 65
Drove Tavern, 19; Murder at, 99;
Noble Heath's School, *ib.*

E

Evans, Joshua, 120, 131, 134, 148;
Randall, 134

F

Flag Tavern, 17
Fish Tavern, 17
Fahnestock, Caspar, 55–56; Sketch
of, 57; Charles, 70, 72; Andrew,
73
French and Indian War, 49
Free Masons, 163

G

Gallagherville Tavern, 23
" Green Tree," 17, 150; Old Hickory Club, 151, 154; Old Milestone, 155; Columbia Railway,
159–163; Peculiarities, 161; Sergeant Wallace, 164; Destroyed
by Fire, 169; Paoli Encampment,
171; Post Office, 172

Metalmark Books is a joint imprint of The Pennsylvania State University
Press and the Office of Digital Scholarly Publishing at The Pennsylvania State
University Libraries. The facsimile editions published under this
imprint are reproductions of out-of-print, public domain works that hold
a significant place in Pennsylvania's rich literary and cultural past.
Metalmark editions are primarily reproduced from the University Libraries'
extensive Pennsylvania collections and in cooperation with other
state libraries. These volumes are available to the public for viewing online
and can be ordered as print-on-demand paperbacks.

LIBRARY OF CONGRESS CATALOGING-IN-PUBLICATION DATA

Sachse, Julius Friedrich, 1842-1919.
The wayside inns on the Lancaster roadside between Philadelphia
and Lancaster / Julius F. Sachse.
p.   cm.
Summary: "Reprint of a 1915 work documenting historic inns and taverns
along the Lancaster Turnpike in Pennsylvania. Includes descriptions of sixty-
two inns, with chapters exploring the history and importance of famous inns
such as the General Warren, Spread Eagle, and Paoli"--Provided by publisher.
Originally published: Lancaster, Pa. : Press of the New Era Printing Co., c1915.
ISBN 978-0-271-05241-0 (paper : alk. paper)
1. Pennsylvania--History, Local. 2. Philadelphia Region (Pa.)--History, Local.
3. Lancaster Region (Pa.)--History, Local. 4. Historic hotels--Pennsylvania. 5.
Historic hotels--Pennsylvania--Philadelphia Region. 6. Historic hotels
--Pennsylvania--Lancaster Region. 7. Taverns (Inns)--Pennsylvania.
8. Taverns (Inns)--Pennsylvania--Philadelphia Region.
9. Taverns (Inns)--Pennsylvania--Lancaster Region.
I. Title.
F150.S14 2011
974.8--dc23
2011026024

Printed in the United States of America
Reprinted by The Pennsylvania State University Press, 2011
University Park, PA 16802-1003

The University Libraries at Penn State and the Penn State University Press,
through the Office of Digital Scholarly Publishing, produced this volume to
preserve the informational content of the original. In compliance with current
copyright law, this reprint edition uses digital technology and is printed on
paper that complies with the permanent Paper Standard issued by the
National Information Standards Organization (ANSI z39.48–1992).